Lecture Notes in
Information Technology

# Multi-agent System Applications:
# On-demand Electric Vehicles
# Dial-a-Ride Operation System

Lecture Notes in
Information Technology

# Multi-agent System Applications: On-demand Electric Vehicles Dial-a-Ride Operation System

Yee Ming Chen

Chi-Shun Hsueh

Bo-Yuan Wang

Published by iConcept Press Limited

Published by iConcept Press Limited

Copyright © iConcept Press 2016

http://www.iconceptpress.com

ISBN: 978-1-922227-508

Printed in the United States of America

# Contents

# Preface

Transportation is one of the industrial sectors most impacted by global climate change. Electric vehicles are energy-efficient and often presented as a zero-emission transport mode to achieve longer-term de-carbonization visions in the transport sector. Governments are recognizing the highest priority of development of public transit policies for sustainability. Taxis are visible and thus electric vehicle use in taxi service can bring attention in urban life to a commitment towards sustainability in the public's opinion. For this reason, this lecture note proposed a multi-agent system (MAS) approach incorporating electric vehicle dial-a-ride (DAR) operation and the appropriate car-pool and car-sharing schemes design for taxi service. The dial-a-ride operation problem consists of designing vehicle routes and schedules for users who specify pick-up and drop-off requests between origins and destinations. We have made some MAS simulation studies, which aims to minimize the total vehicle-distance travelled subject to meeting all advanced customers' requests, and constraints on vehicle capacity, pickup/ delivery time-window, customer ride-time and battery-charging restrictions. In this study, we designed vehicle dial-a-ride operation system and algorithm development for dynamic variants of electric vehicles DAR, to enable on-line simulations of realistic scale for on-demand transit. We will also investigate robust solution approaches for the stochastic electric vehicles DAR. The insights obtained in studying these electric vehicles DAR variants would help to build an integrated planning model for location of charging stations and on-demand transit request management. This lecture note is expected to be read by academics (i.e. teachers, researchers and students), technology solutions developers and enterprise managers. The authors are expecting that the lecture note will contribute to the MAS technological concept in other applications. Finally, the authors are grateful to support and sponsor by the Ministry of Science and Technology, R.O.C., under project number MOST 104-2918-I-155-001.

Yee Ming Chen
*Department of Industrial Engineering and Management*
*Yuan Ze University*
*Taiwan, R.O.C.*

Chi-Shun Hsueh
*Information and Communication Research Division*
*National Chung Shan Institute and Technology*
*Taiwan, R.O.C.*

Bo-Yuan Wang
*Innovation Development Center (IDC)*
*Department of Industrial Engineering and Management*
*Yuan Ze University*
*Taiwan, R.O.C.*

# 1

# Introduction

## 1.1 Background

With the progress of economics plus the development of industry and commerce, various energy and environment issues appear. Particularly, energy crisis and global warming are the most important problems. And researchers and experts find out the causes of these two problems are the emission of $CO_2$ and energy overuse (Wikipedia, 2009; Antle, J. *et al.*, 2001). Many experts, scholars and industrials are looking for the solution to deal with these kinds of problems. On the other hand, the environment destruction makes people realize that using the resources with unconstraint can destroy the balance of natural environment and people (顧洋, 2005). The only way is to ensure the sustainable development of ecological environment and let environment can stably coexisting with people. So far, many countries held many conventions to conclude and sign contracts to protect the earth (such as Basel Convention, Kyoto Protocol, Montreal Protocol on Substances that Deplete the Ozone Layer and so on). In the world, each type of industry tries to find out a good way (e.g.: substitute, renewable energy and so on) to save energy and reduce the generation of $CO_2$.

Among all of industries, transportation industry quite cares about the energy crisis and global warming problems (Seow, K.T. *et al.*, 2008; http://e-info.org.tw/taxonomy/term/17123, 2015; http://www.epd.gov. hk/epd/partnership/chi/tran.htm, 2014). There are many types of transportation in metropolis, for example, taxi, bus, Mass Rapid Transit (MRT), train, airplane, etc (http://tw.knowledge.yahoo.com/question/question?qid=1405122412364, 2015). Each type of transportation provides various services to satisfy passengers' requirements. With development and advancement of technology, the service quality of transportation has significantly been improved (Wu, C.C., 2006; Seow, K.T. *et al.*, 2008).

Private vehicle is one of the transportation who generates a lot of CO2 and uses much of energy (Chao, C.C., 2009). Moreover, for many years, Due to the deterioration of energy crisis and global warming, mass transportation (such as train, bus, MRT, etc.) becomes more important than before for metropolis. Among the all kinds of transportations, taxi is a unique transportation. It has the features of high flexibility and efficiency (Wu, C.C., 2006). So taxi plays an important role in the transportation system of metropolis. On the other hand, with the revolution of technology, vehicle can be driven by electricity. Hence, electric taxi (e-taxi) comes with the tide of fashion (Wu, C.C., 2006; Seow, K.T. *et al.*, 2008; http://en. wikipedia.org/wiki/Taxicab, 2015). Due to the importance of electric taxi, it has attracted many researchers to study the management issues.

There are two main types of transportation problems: Pick-up and deliver (PDP) and dial-a-ride (DAR) (Kok, I.D. & Lucassen, T., 2007). Many researchers apply some approaches to try to solve these problems. Heuristic algorithm and simulation are the most common research approaches. In simulation field, more and more researchers apply multi-agent technique to solve these problems more efficiently (Kok, I.D. & Lucassen, T., 2007; Siebers, P.O. *et al.*, 2008).

## 1.2    Motives

### 1.2.1    The Importance of Electric-taxi

To resist global warming, mass transportation plays an important role in metropolis. Public can travel by taking mass transportation rather than driving a car. In this way, public can reduce the $CO_2$ generation and air pollution. But in order to reduce the operation cost of mass transportation, transportation company has to abandon the flexibility and efficiency. However taxi just compensates the disadvantages of mass transportation, because it has the features of high flexibility and efficiency.

In addition to global warming, gas and gasoline consumption also causes air pollution. Moreover high fuel cost and the decrease of passenger number that caused by the reduction of public income (the reduction of public income that resulted from economics depression) can reduce the taxi company's revenue (http://www.greenparty.org.tw/division.php?itemid=831, 2015). So, electric taxi comes with the tide of fashion. Electric taxi means a taxi is driven by electricity. It has many advantages. For the earth, electric taxi can reduce the air pollution and global warming, because it can't emit $CO_2$. For taxi driver, electric taxi can reduce the fuel cost, due to the cost of replenishing electricity is lower than gas or gasoline. Hence electric taxi is an important transportation for metropolises.

Contrary, electric-taxi also has disadvantage. The worst disadvantage in electric-taxi is the electricity that's also the biggest limitation. During the electric-taxi traveling period, the electricity of taxi is decreasing. When the electricity of electric-taxi is not enough to support next passenger service or longer traveling, electric-taxi has to replenish its' electricity in the electric station like refueling in gas station to vehicles. So during the replenishing period, electric-taxi can't do any service and passenger still waits for service. Under this condition, that will cause the reduction of taxi company's revenue and passenger satisfaction. However, revenue and passenger satisfaction are the most important performance measures for taxi company. So electric-taxi company has to propose some replenishing management policies to deal with the electric replenishing problem. Hence how to manage the electric replenishing problem of electric-taxi becomes a very important issue for taxi company. And that's also one of our research purposes.

### 1.2.2    The Importance of Dial-a-ride System

So far, most of passengers stand beside road and wait for a taxi. In this condition, there are some disadvantages. First, passenger doesn't know how long he/she has to wait until a taxi passes by. Second, passenger is not sure the coming taxi is free or not. So passenger will be late for dating or work. Besides, taxi needs to go around and looks for passenger. But the most of operation time, taxi is idle. Hence the operation utility is too low to cause the energy waste. Contrary, dial-a-ride system is a good solution to solve this problem. Using this kind of service system, passenger can call for a free taxi to taxi service center but doesn't need to wait longer than before. And driver can save the taxi energy by stopping beside the road and waits for an order that comes from service center. So driver doesn't have to go around and look for passenger. Hence, DAR system is very important in taxi operation system.

As mentioned above, our research will focus on the electric taxi DAR operation system.

### 1.2.3    The Reason of Choosing Multi-agent Technique

Our research will apply multi-agent technique to simulate and analyze the vehicle DAR operation system. Following, we specify the reason of choosing multi-agent technique as our simulation approach.

First, we describe the reason of choosing simulation as our research approach. There are three main research approaches: Analytics, heuristic algorithm and simulation (Kok, I.D. & Lucassen, T., 2007; Siebers, P.O. *et al.*, 2008). Among these research approaches, simulation is used to observe the development and changes of a system over time. And simulation can be used to construct the behavior of system, so researcher can observe the interaction and phenomena within system operation via the simulation (Kok, I.D. & Lucassen, T., 2007; Siebers, P.O. *et al.*, 2008). One of our main research purposes is to observe and discuss the phenomena of vehicle DAR operation system, plus the phenomena of vehicle DAR operation system can be easily presented by applying simulation approach. Therefore we identified the simulation as our research approach.

Second, we describe the reason of choosing multi-agent technique as our simulation approach. Computer simulation has been used in many research areas since the 1960s. According to literature review, we list the good reasons for choosing computer simulation (Kok, I.D. & Lucassen, T., 2007; Seow, K.T. *et al.*, 2008; Siebers, P.O. *et al.*, 2008):

1. The physical system is not available: Often, computer simulations are used to determine whether or not a system should ever be built; so obviously, experimentation is out of the question.

2. The experiment may be dangerous: Often, simulations are performed in order to find out whether the real experiment might 'blow-up', placing the experimenter and/or the equipment under danger of injury/damage or death/destruction (for example, an atomic reactor, or an aircraft flown by an inexperienced person for training purposes).

3. The cost of experimentation is too high: Often, simulations are used when real experiments are too expensive.

4. The time constants of the system are not compatible with those of the experimenter: Often, simulations are performed because the real experiment executes so quickly that it can hardly be observed (for example, an explosion), or because the real experiment executes so slowly that the experimenter is long dead before the experiment is completed. Simulations allow us to speed up or slow down experiments at will.

5. Control variables, and/or system parameters may be inaccessible: Often, computer simulations are performed because they allow us to access all input (variables), whereas, in the real system, some inputs may not be accessible for manipulation.

There are three main computer simulation approaches: Discrete event simulation, system dynamics and multi-agent technique. Among these simulation approaches, multi-agent technique becomes common and popular in the early of 1990s. And there are some important features of multi-agent technique to help us understand why we apply multi-agent technique as our simulation approach: autonomy, social ability, reactivity, pro-activeness, adaptability, mobility and temporal continuity (Kok, I.D. & Lucassen, T., 2007; Siebers, P.O. *et al.*, 2008). Obviously, these features of multi-agent technique can help researcher to more properly construct and present the behaviors of vehicle DAR operation system (Jiang, B., 2000; Kok, I.D. & Lucassen, T., 2007; Seow, K.T. *et al.*, 2008; Siebers, P.O. *et al.*, 2008). So the multi-agent technique is the most suitable simulation approach for our research.

## 1.3    The Purpose of Research

This research aims at applying multi-agent technique to simulate and analyze the vehicle DAR operation system. The purposes of this research are:

1. To manage and observe the vehicle DAR operation simulation system.

2. To analyze and discuss the simulation of vehicle DAR operation system with case study.

3.  To construct graphic user interface (GUI) to connect with on-line.

## 1.4    Research Structure

The structure of this research is diagramed as Figure 1.1. First of all, we briefly describe the background of research, motives, purposes of research, research structure and research constraints in the introduction. Especially, we also specify the reason of choosing multi-agent technique in this chapter. We will collect literatures and specify the current research condition of vehicle DAR operation system and multi-agent in the literature review. Then we follow each step of research method to construct the vehicle DAR operation simulation system and describe the detail of each step in research method. Later, we construct the scenarios of vehicle DAR operation system with case study. And then we will analyze the data collected form the simulation of vehicle DAR operation system. Finally, we make a summary based on the analysis results and describe the follow-up researches in the final chapter.

## 1.5    Research Constraints

Due to the real vehicle DAR operation system is too complicated. In order to facilitate the simulation of vehicle DAR operation system, we simplify the real vehicle DAR operation system. So the data of vehicle DAR operation system is virtue. In other words, it is difficult to obtain the real data related to the vehicle DAR operation system. In order to make the simulation easily operate with real world, we will construct a Graphic User Interface to validate and modify the simulation with on-line later.

## 1.6    Research Method

The research method of this research is diagramed as Figure 1.2. The detail of each step of this research method will be explained in chapter 3. The research method is divided into two phases. Phase 1 is to construct the vehicle DAR operation simulation system. Phase 2 is to add the management policies establishment. Finally, we construct GUI to modify and validate with on-line.

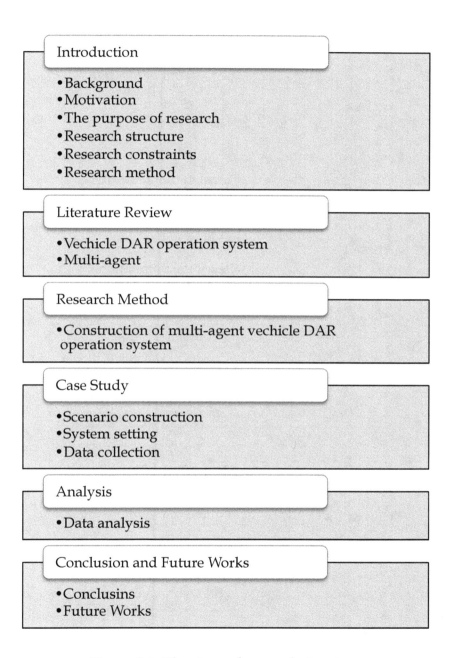

**Figure 1.1:** The steps of research structure.

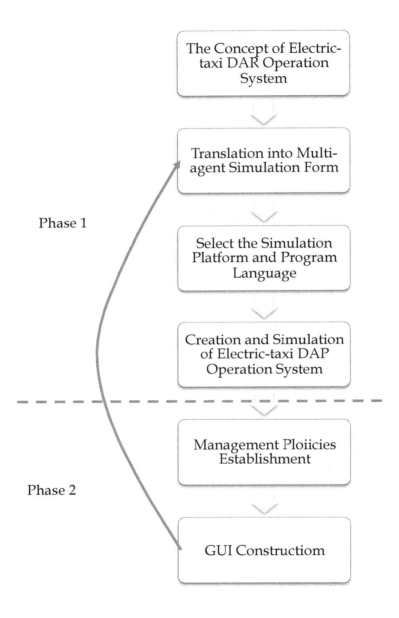

**Figure 1.2:** The steps of research method.

# 2

# Literature Review

## 2.1 Vehicle DAR operation system

### 2.1.1 Definition of Vehicle DAR Operation System

First of all, we need to specify the vehicle DAR operation system. Vehicle DAR operation system is defined as that passenger uses calls for service to service center, then service center orders a vehicle to pick passenger up and deliver to his/her destination. Passenger, service center and vehicle use wireless device (for example: Mobile phone, radio and so on) as their communication tool (Wu, C.C., 2006; Kok, I.D. & Lucassen, T., 2007; Seow, K.T., 2008; http://en.wikipedia.org/wiki/Taxicab, 2014).

### 2.1.2 The Framework of Vehicle DAR Operation System

The framework of vehicle DAR operation system is diagramed as Figure 2.1. Vehicle DAR operation system is consisted of passengers, service center, communication tool, vehicles and environment. The detail of each element is described as follows (Wu, C.C., 2006; Seow, K.T. *et al.*, 2008; Kok, I.D. & Lucassen, T., 2007; http://en.wikipedia.org/wiki/Taxicab, 2015).

1. Passengers: A person who will use communication tool to send requirements to service center. The main information includes current location, destination and so on.

2. Service center: A center (like taxi control center) which will integrate all of the information obtained from passengers, vehicles and environment. And then the center will send order to a vehicle to perform task.

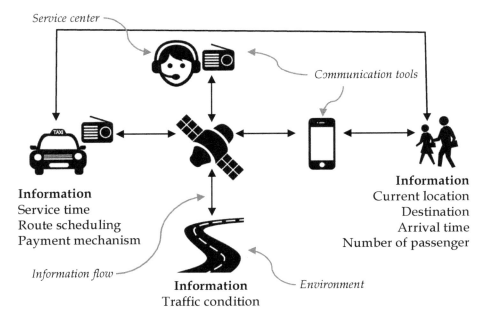

**Figure 2.1:** The framework of vehicle DAR operation system.

3.  Communication tools: The tool (like mobile phone, radio and so on) which will help service center, passenger and vehicle to deliver their message or information.

4.  Vehicles: The vehicle (like taxi) which will perform the task ordered from service center

5.  Environment: The Environment (like road) which will change its' state over time (like traffic jam or spacious).

### 2.1.3    The Features of Vehicle DAR Operation System

There are three main features of vehicle DAR operation system. First is fast, every vehicle can deliver passengers to their destinations with fast speed. Second is convenient, there are many locations of vehicle around the metropolises, so it is very convenient for public. Third is comfortable, each vehicle provides comfortable interior facilities. Make public feel better during their travel (Wu, C.C., 2006; Seow, K.T., 2008; http://en. wikipedia.org/wiki/Taxicab, 2015).

### 2.1.4    The Research Review of Vehicle DAR Operation System

According to the literature review, this paper listed ten main characteristics (see Table 2.1). And these characteristics are considerable for vehicle DAR operation system (Cubillos C, Polanco FG et al, 2008a). Moreover, we distinguish our method from those existing methods in literature review. Obviously, these existing methods are incomplete in vehicle DAR operation system. So these shortages can be the improvements of our electric-taxi DAR operation simulation.

## 2.2    Multi-agent System

### 2.2.1    Definition of Multi-agent

The concept of agent was introduced in computer science during the early 90s and multi-agent systems (MAS) soon attracted the interest of researchers far beyond the traditional computer science (Ali, W., 2006; Siebers, P.O., 2008; Ezzedine, H., 2005).

There are many different definition of agent in the academic community. Briefly, an agent is defined as an entity that could interact with environment. "Interact" means an entity could perceive the changes of environment or other entities by sensor and act on the environment or other entities by actuator, update the knowledge and learn constantly. Besides interacting based on agent's decision rule (Siebers, P.O., 2008; Kok, I.D., 2007). Multi-agent is defined as the set of agents. Just like human, each agent has specific goal or task. And they will cooperate with others.

### 2.2.2    The Framework of Multi-agent

The framework of agent is illustrated as Figure 2.2. The framework of agent is consisted of sensor, knowledge base, decision rules and actuator. The detail of these five elements is specified as follows (Ali, W., 2006; Siebers, P.O., 2008).

1. **Sensor** which can help agent perceive the changes of environment, so that agent will know what happened in the real or virtual world.

2. **Knowledge base** that will update the information captured from sensor to keep the information is up to date.

| Characteristics | Ezzedine H, Kolski C and Pe'ninou A (2005) | Lansdowne A (2006) | Kok ID and Lucassen, T (2007) | Cubillos C, Polanco FG and Demartini C (2008)[b] | Seow KT, Dang NH and Lee DH (2008) | Galus M et al, (2009) | Our proposed method |
|---|---|---|---|---|---|---|---|
| 1. Being generic | * | * | * | * | * | * | * |
| 2. Being agent-based simulation | * | * | * | * | * | * | * |
| 3. Multiple (people) to multiple (cars) simulation | * | * | * | * | * | * | * |
| 4. Taking into account the energy wasting of cars | | | | | | * | * |
| 5. Taking into account the change of cars' velocity | | * | | | | | * |
| 6. Information management de-centralization | * | * | * | * | | * | |
| 7. Hybrid information management (Combining centralization and decentralization) | | | | | * | | * |
| 8. Taking into account traffic jam | | * | | | | * | * |
| 9. The traffic jam management (such as allowing cars move that excludes the road which is under traffic jam) | | * | | | | | * |
| 10. Allowing cars move based on shortest path | | | * | | * | | * |

**Table 2.1:** Criteria distinguishing our method from those existing in literature review.

3. **Decision rules** that are the selection rules of agent actions. They only execute the actions that conforms the decision rules.

4. **Actuator** which can execute the actions what agent wants to do.

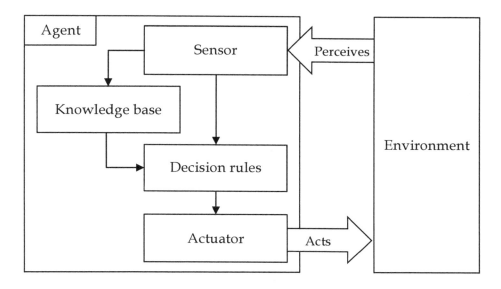

**Figure 2.2**: The framework of Agent.

The framework of multi-agent is diagramed as Figure 2.3. In Figure 2.3, container A, B and C represent three different types of agents. Each type of container includes many agents. Every agent has his own goal and can interact with each other and other agents those are included in other containers.

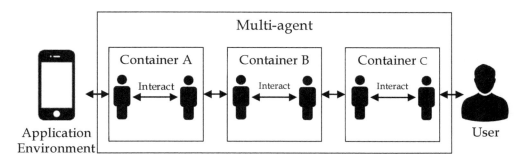

**Figure 2.3**: The framework of Multi-agent.

### 2.2.3   The Features of Agent

In general, agent possesses some important features, these features can help agent perform a task or a job. This sub-section list seven main features of agent as follows. Some agents may have all of the features, but some are not (Ali, W., 2006; Siebers, P.O., 2008; Ezzedine, H., 2005; Kok, I.D., 2007).

1. Autonomy: After assigning a task to an agent. Agents operate without the direct intervention of human or others, and have some kind of control over their actions and internal states.

2. Social ability: Agents can interact with other agents via some kind of agent-communication language (ACL).

3. Reactivity: Agents perceive the changes of environment or what happened, (which may be the physical world, a user via a graphical user interface, a collection of other agents, the Internet, or perhaps all of these combined) and respond in a timely fashion.

4. Pro-activeness: Agents do not simply act in response to their environment; they are able to exhibit goal-directed behavior by taking the initiative.

5. Adaptability: Agents can adjust their state with the changes of time and environment and learn through the result of identifying behavior.

6. Mobility: Agents can move to other environments with data or information. They can move by scheduling or their intentions.

7. Temporal continuity: Agents can do any types of action with resources what they have during the task period.

# 3

# Research Method

## 3.1 Electric-taxi DAR Operation System

In this chapter, we describe the electric-taxi DAR operation system (Figure 3. 1). We divide the electric-taxi DAR operation system into three parts. First part is the agent container. In agent container, we have six kinds of agents: electric-taxis, control center, passengers, electric stations, road and stops. Agents are divided into two types (Figure 3.2). First type is active agents those have their own structures and behaviors. Second type is passive agents those only have their structures. The specification of each type of agent is as follows:

1. Passive Agents (PA): This category of agents represents entities that have a structure, without a behavior. Usually, a large part of the elements contained in the simulation environment belongs to this category.

2. Active agents (AA): This category of agents represents entities, which have structures and behaviors: These entities actively participate in the simulation. For this category, we must specify the data structures of the entities (spatial and non-spatial structures) as well as their behaviors (spatial and non-spatial behaviors).

The second part is environment. Environment is composed of time container, data container, event container and scenario container. Time container includes all of the related information and variables. Data container contains all of the related information and variables to support data analysis. Event container has many events to be the triggers of every possible action of each agent. We also design three kinds of scenarios in the

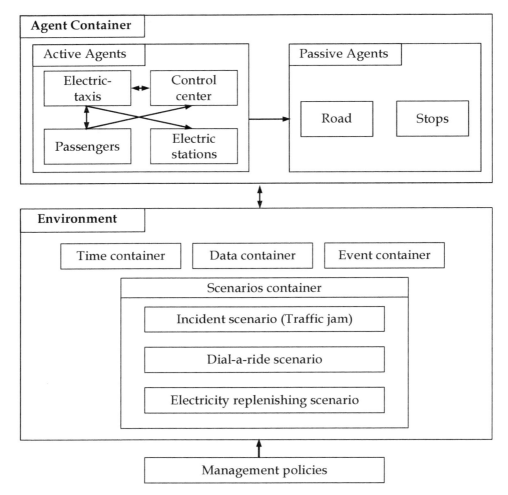

**Figure 3.1:** The framework of electric-taxi DAR operation system.

| Passive agent | |
|---|---|
| Structure | |
| Non-spatial Structure | Spatial Structure (2D) |

| Active agent | |
|---|---|
| Structure | |
| Non-spatial Structure | Spatial Structure |
| Behavior | |
| Non-spatial Structure | Spatial Structure (2D) |

**Figure 3.2:** Passive Agents and Active agents.

scenario container: Incident management (traffic jam), dial-a-ride management and electricity replenishing management.

Third part, we will design management policies to manage the electric-taxi DAR operation simulation system in the Section 4.In this section, we will specify the framework of active agents which belong to agent container and the scenario interaction processes of scenario container in the environment.

Following, we specify the each step of research method and follow the step to construct the electric-taxi DAR operation simulation system. The detail will be described later. Following, we briefly describe the each step of research method.

### 3.1.1    Step 1: The Concept of Electric-taxi DAR Operation system

Simulations are generally used to support decision making. In simulation applications, decisions are influenced by the features of the simulated phenomenon and environment. Before developing a multi-agent simulation, we must study concept of electric-taxi DAR operation system. This step is very important because it helps us to identify the entities and scenario of the simulation. Identifying the scenario to be simulated and environment is a very important task, because it facilitates the translating into multi-agent simulation form of step 2. This also can help to reduce the level of complexity by reducing the size of the phenomenon to be simulated or the complexity of the simulation environment.

### 3.1.2    Step 2: Translating into Multi-agent Simulation Form

We must translate the concept of electric-taxi DAR operation system into multi-agent simulation form. This step is very important; because we can follow the multi-agent simulation form to create simulate the electric-taxi DAR operation system in next step.

In this step of the research method, we distinguish two types of agents (see Figure 3.3):

1.  Passive Agents (PA): This category of agents represents entities that have a structure, without a behavior. Usually, a large part of the elements contained in the simulation environment belongs to this category.

| Passive agent | |
|---|---|
| Structure | |
| Non-spatial Structure | Spatial Structure (2D) |

| Active agent | |
|---|---|
| Structure | |
| Non-spatial Structure | Spatial Structure |
| Behavior | |
| Non-spatial Behavior | Spatial Behavior (2D) |

**Figure 3.3:** Passive agent and Active Agent.

2. Active agents (AA): This category of agents represents entities, which have structures and behaviors: These entities actively participate in the simulation. For this category, we must specify the data structures of the entities (spatial and non-spatial structures) as well as their behaviors (spatial and non-spatial behaviors).

### 3.1.3    Step 3: Select the Simulation Platform and Program Language

Before we create and simulate the electric-taxi DAR operation system, we have to select the software agent simulation environment and standard language.

1. To use an existing software agent simulation environment such as NetLogo, AnyLogic etc. In our electric-taxi DAR operation system, we choose the Anylogic software agent simulation environment which be used to construct the simulation model.

2. To using an existing standard language, such as C, C++ or Java for example. In our electric-taxi DAR operation system, we select the Java language which be used to write the program of simulation model.

### 3.1.4    Step 4: Creation and Simulation of Electric-taxi DAR Operation System

In this step, first, we use the multi-agent simulation form to create the electric-taxi DAR operation system simulation in the selected platform and language. Second, we perform the simulation on the selected simulation platform. Third, we use some statistic diagram to analyze the data that obtained from the simulation. And make a brief conclusion to explain what the meaning of the data for electric-taxi DAR operation system.

### 3.1.5    Step 5: Management Policies Establishment

In this step, we will set up many management policies in our electric-taxi DAR operation simulation system and simulation with the case study which in the chapter 4.

### 3.1.6    Step 6: GUI Construction

Construct GUI to validate and modified the electric-taxi DAR operation simulation system with on-line.

Following, we follow the steps that mentioned above, and practice the research method for creating the electric-taxi DAR operation simulation system.

## 3.2    The Concept of Electric-taxi DAR Operation System

This paper aims to the application of agent-based simulation on the field of electric-taxi DAR operation system with a view towards raising passenger satisfaction. It can allow one to assess, in advance, whether a scheme is likely to work, and how well it compares to other alternatives. Before simulation, we have to identify the concept of the concept of electric-taxi DAR operation system to help us to construct the electric-taxi DAR operation simulation system later.

The Figure 3.4 is illustrating the concept of electric-taxi DAR operation system. From the Figure 3.4, we can induce the basic simulation scenario and main simulation entities as follows: The five main entities of the concept of electric-taxi DAR operation system are passengers, electric-taxis, supply site, road and control center. The basic scenario: Passenger will give a call to control center and tell them what his requirement is. And then control center assign a vehicle to pick him up and deliver him to his destination. During the traveling period, each electric-taxi will deliver the road information to each other to support them making decision (whether driver change road or not). If the road which electric-taxi is approaching

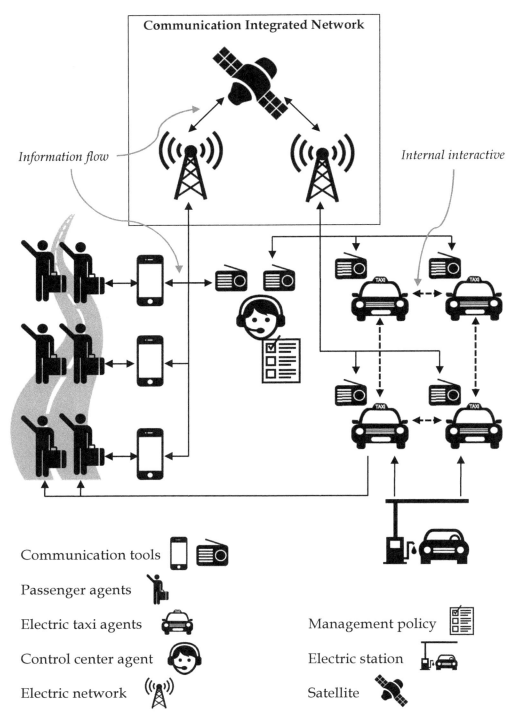

**Figure 3.4:** The concept of electric-taxi DAR operation system.

and the state of road is jam-packed, in order to avoid getting in traffic jam, the driver will find another road to move on according road information. During the operation period, driver will check his electric-taxi electricity and decide whether he needs to replenish electricity or not. During the replenishment period, electric-taxi will deliver related supply site information to each vehicle. The "thin line" represents the information sending flow, and its' arrow represent the information sending direction and object. The " thick line" represents the internal interaction of electric-taxis, and its' arrow represent the interaction direction and object. The "book" represents different management policies.

## 3.3    Translating into Multi-agent Simulation Form

### 3.3.1    The Illustration of Scenarios and Entities

After understanding the basic concept of electric-taxi DAR operation system. We identify the scenario of the electric-taxi DAR operation system, and find out the basic scenario are consisted of three parts: First is incident management scenario (traffic jam), second is electric vehicle replenishing electricity scenario and third is electric-taxi DAR scenario. The structure of basic scenario is diagramed as Figure 3.5.

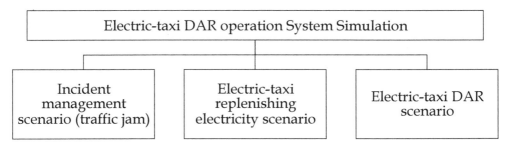

**Figure 3.5:** The electric-taxi DAR operation system simulation scenarios.

Figure 3.6 is to illustrate the main simulation entities. There are five types of simulation entities: Road, passengers, electric-taxis, supply site and control center. the blue liner represents the interaction between entities. Following, we change the five conceptual entities into a multi-agent

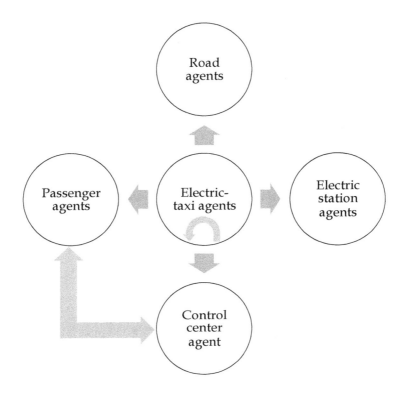

**Figure 3.6:** Entities of electric taxi DAR operation system.

simulation form. So in our multi-agent simulation, we define the passenger, control center and vehicle as active agents. On the other hand, we define the road and supply site as passive agent.

### 3.3.2    The Illustration of Framework of Each Type of Agent

Following, we will describe the framework of each type of agent and define each function that within the framework of agent. The functions within the framework of agent:

1.  K: Knowledge base of the agent. Knowledge of the agent can help agent make decision more precisely.

2.  IS: Information source. Information source means the information where comes form.

3.  R: Response. Response means the object of action.

4.  D: Decision rules. Decision means the alternatives, mechanisms or algorithm to help agent make proper actions or decisions.

5.  In this section, we illustrate four kinds of agents:

6.  CCA: Control center agent.

7.  PA: Passenger agents.

8.  TA: Electric Taxi agents.

9.  EA: Electric station agents.

First, we enumerate some examples to help understanding the meaning of each function in the framework of agent. In Figure 3.7, for perceiving, we use IS-TA to represent that control center agent perceives the information (IS) that comes form electric-taxi agents (TA). For knowledge, we use K-TA to represent that control center agent owns the knowledge (K) about electric-taxi agents (TA). For decision, we use D-T to represent that control center agent owns the decision mechanism (D) about electric-taxi agents (T). For action, we use R-TA to represent that control center agent responses (R) to electric-taxi agents (TA). The rest can be deduced by analogy. Following, we specify the framework of each type of agent.

The framework of the control center agent is diagramed as Figure 3.7. In the framework of control center agent, there are three kinds of information source: Simulation environment, passenger agents and taxi agents. For control center agent, it has four kinds of knowledge: the information about electric-taxi agents, road, electric station, animation parameters and its' attributes. Combine the knowledge and information that perceived, and as the input data of decisions. There are four decision rules: Passenger service rule, Taxi chosen rule, Stop chosen rule and Electric station chosen rule. Through decision rules, control center agent execute proper actions to two kinds of agents: Electric-taxi agents and passenger agents. Finally, the behavior of control center agent will be displayed on the screen via animation parameters.

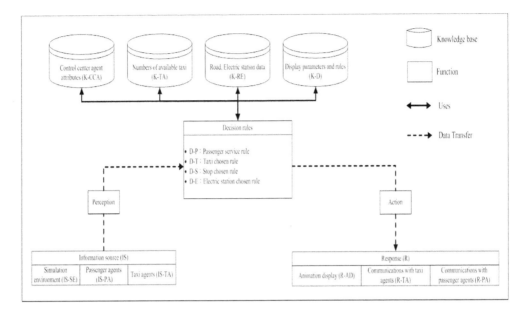

**Figure 3.7:** The framework of Control Center agent.

The framework of the passenger agent is diagramed as Figure 3.8. In the framework of passenger agents, there are three kinds of information source: Simulation environment, control center agent and electric-taxi agents. For passenger agents, it has two kinds of knowledge: The information about its' attributes and animation parameters. Combine the knowledge and information that perceived, and as the input data of decisions. There is one decision rule: Calling rule Through decision rules, passenger agents execute proper actions to two kinds of agents: electric-taxi agents and control center agents. Finally, the behavior of passenger agents will be displayed on the screen via animation parameters.

The framework of electric-taxi agent is diagramed as Figure 3.9. In the framework of electric-taxi agent, there are four kinds of information source: Simulation environment, passenger agents, control center agent and other electric-taxi agents. For electric-taxi agent, it has three kinds of knowledge: The information about road, electric station, animation parameters and its' attributes. Combine the knowledge and information that perceived, and as the input data of decisions. There are five decision rules: Shortest path searching rules, Avoid traffic jam rules, Electric station

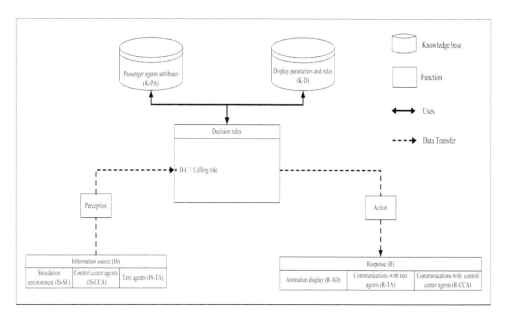

**Figure 3.8:** The framework of Passenger agent

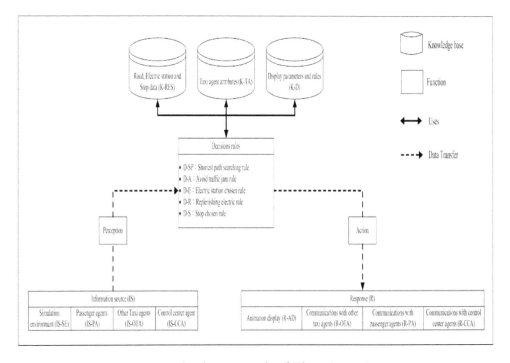

**Figure 3.9:** The framework of Electric-taxi agent.

chosen rules, Replenishing electric rules and Stop chosen rules. Through decision rules, taxi agent executes proper actions to three kinds of agents: Other electric-taxi agents, control center agent and passenger agents. Finally, the behavior of taxi agent will be displayed on the screen via animation parameters.

The framework of the electric station agent is diagramed as Figure 3.10. In the framework of electric station agent, there is one kind of information source: electric-taxi agents. For electric station agent, it has two kinds of knowledge: The information about its' attributes and animation parameters. Combine the knowledge and information that perceived, and as the input data of decisions. There is one decision rule: Update state and data. Through decision rules, taxi agent executes proper actions to one kind of agents: Electric-taxi agents. Finally, the behavior of electric station agent will be displayed on the screen via animation parameters.

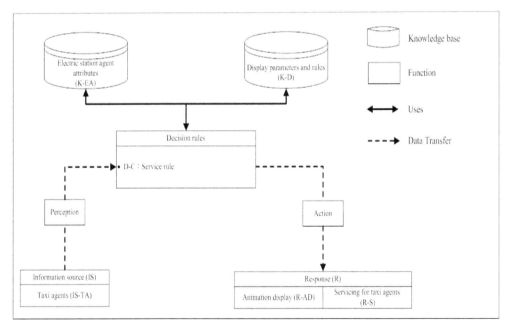

**Figure 3.10:** The framework of Electric station agent.

### 3.3.3    The Electric-taxi Agents' Interaction Processes Diagram

As mentioned in section 3.2.1, we divide the electric-taxi DAR operation system into three parts of scenario. In this sub-section, we will specify the agents' interaction process of each scenario. The three agents' interaction processes are: (1) Dial-a-ride and deliver interaction process (2) traffic jam management interaction process (3) electricity replenishing interaction process. The detail of each agents' interaction process is described as follows.

Figure 3.11 is the dial-a-ride interaction process diagram. In the electric-taxi agents' interaction processes diagram, a rectangle represents an actor that also means the executor of an event/behavior. The dotted line represents the state of actor is static, that means actor doesn't do any action. The straight thick line represents the state of actor is dynamic with time. The length of straight thick line represents how long the behavior/event will last. The transverse thick line represents an event/behavior is executed. The arrow of transverse thick line represents the interaction object of an event/behavior execution. Final, the number which is in front of every event/behavior represents the execution sequence.

In this dial-a-ride interaction process, there are three agents: Control center, electric-taxis and passengers. The detail of process is described as below: In the beginning user execute the simulation (step1). Immediately, simulation initial and generate three kind of agent (step2-1, 2-3, 2-4 and 2-5), and simulation time is begin running and updating (step2-2). After generating, control center and electric-taxi stand by for passenger demand (step3-1 and 3-2). On the other hand, passenger sends a requirement to control center and waiting for response (step3-3). Control center assign a most suitable taxi for passenger and stand by for next demand (step4, 5-1 and 5-2). Then assigned-electric-taxi finds the shortest path to move to pick passenger up (step6, 7 and 8). After arriving at passenger location, electric-taxi delivers passenger to his destination (step9-1 and 9-2). When traveling finished, electric-taxi stand by in the current position as well as passenger gets off and leave the system (step10-1 and 10-2).

Table 3.1 and 3.2 is the specification of non-spatial and spatial structure and behavior of each type of agent in dial-a-ride interaction scenario. In this traffic jam management interaction process (Figure 3.12); there is one type of agents: Electric-taxis. The detail of process is described as

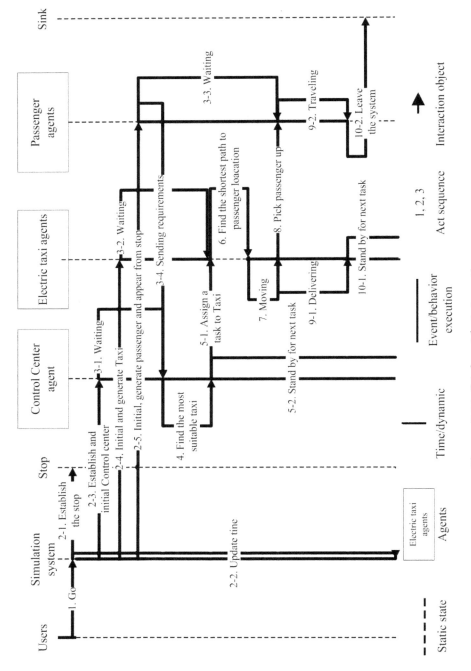

**Figure 3.11:** Dial-a-ride interaction process.

| Duty / Goal | Non-spatial behavior | Non-spatial structure | |
|---|---|---|---|
| | | Variables | Functions |
| 1. Process passenger requirements and road data | 1. Select passenger according to passenger selection mechanism() | 1. Color | 1. Setting color function() |
| 2. Animation | 2. Receive passenger requirements and information | 2. Road database | 2. Taxi selection function() |
| | 3. Sending order to taxi | 3. Taxis database | 3. Passenger selection function() |
| | 4. Sending related road data to taxi | 4. Passenger database | 4. Perceive function() |
| | 5. Sending related taxi data to taxi | | 5. Action function() |
| | 6. Assign a taxi to a passenger according to taxi selection mechanism | | 6. Information process function() |
| | 7. Update all of the taxis state | | 7. Update taxi function() |
| | | | 8. Update passenger function() |
| | | | 9. Update road function() |

**Table 3.1A** The specification of non-spatial structure and behavior of Control Center in dial-a-ride scenario.

| Duty / Goal | Non-spatial behavior | Non-spatial structure | |
|---|---|---|---|
| | | Variables | Functions |
| 1. Satisfy his/her demands | 1. Sending a requirement to control center | 1. Color | 1. Setting color function() |
| | | | 2. Setting Id function() |
| | | | 3. Perceive function() |
| | | 2. Id | 4. Action function() |
| 2. Animation | 2. Receive the response from control center | 3. Waiting time record | 5. Record waiting time function() |
| | 3. Waiting for a assigned taxi | 4. Service time record | 6. Record servicing time function() |
| | 4. Get on a car | 5. Whether chosen or not | 7. Update chosen state function() |
| | 5. Get off a car | 6. Whether satisfied or not | 8. Modified the current state function() |

**Table 3.1B** The specification of non-spatial structure and behavior of Passengers in dial-a-ride scenario.

| Duty / Goal | Non-spatial behavior | Non-spatial structure | |
|---|---|---|---|
| | | Variables | Functions |
| 1. Pick passenger up and deliver to destination | 1. Receive order from control center. | 1. Id | 1. Setting color function() |
| | 2. Find the shortest path to move on to passenger location | 2. Color | 2. Setting Id function() |
| | 3. Find the shortest path to move on to passenger destination | 3. Idle or Busy | 3. Perceive function() |
| | 4. Pick passenger up | 4. Busy time record Idle time record | 4. Action function() |
| 2. Animation | 2. Leave the passenger | 5. Whether chosen or not | 5. Shortest path selection function() |
| | | 6. Which road vehicle is moving on | 6. Record Busy time function() |
| | | | 7. Record Idle time function() |
| | | | 8. Update chosen state function() |
| | | | 9. Modified taxi current state function() |
| | | | 10. Update chosen road data function() |

**Table 3.1C** The specification of non-spatial structure and behavior of Electric Taxis in dial-a-ride scenario.

| Agent | Duty / Goal | Non-spatial behavior | Non-spatial structure | |
|-------|-------------|----------------------|----------------------|---|
| | | | Variables | Functions |
| Control center | 1. Process passenger requirements and road data | | 1. x coordinate | 1. Setting x_y position function() |
| | 2. Animation | | 2. y coordinate | |
| Passengers | 1. Satisfy his/her demands | | 1. x coordinate | 1. Setting passenger location function() |
| | 2. Animation | | 2. y coordinate | 2. Setting passenger destination function() |
| Electric-taxis | 1. Pick passenger up and deliver to destination | 1. Decide taxi initial location | 1. x coordinate | 1. Setting taxi location function() |
| | | | 2. y coordinate | 2. Setting taxi velocity function() |
| | | 2. Moving to passenger location | 3. x velocity | 3. Modified taxi velocity function() |
| | 2. Animation | 3. Moving to passenger destination | 4. y velocity | 4. Stop taxi function() |

**Table 3.2** The specification of spatial structure and behavior of each type of agent in dial-a-ride scenario.

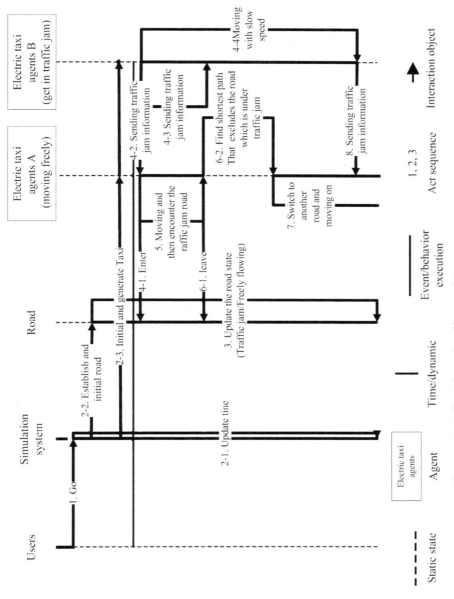

**Figure 3.12:** Incident (traffic jam) interaction process.

below: In the beginning user execute the simulation (step1). Immediately, simulation initial and generate two kind of actors (step2-2 and 2-3), and simulation time is begin running and updating (step2-1). During the simulation period, road will update its' state (traffic jam/ freely flowing) (step3). After generating and simulating for a while, electric-taxi can be divided into two kind of electric-taxis: Some electric-taxis are getting in traffic jam and others are moving freely (represented by the longest transverse thick-line). The electric-taxis those are getting in traffic jam send traffic jam information to each other and other electric-taxis those are not getting traffic jam (step4-2, 4-3 and 4-4). When electric-taxis enter in or leave road, the state of road will be changed into jam-packed or uncrowded (step4-1 and 6-1). When electric-taxi moves to a traffic jam road, driver will find another shortest path that excluded the traffic jam road (step5 and 6-2). And then electric-taxi will switch into another road and move on (step7). Finally, when electric-taxis that are leaving the traffic jam road, they will sending the traffic jam information again (step8).

Table 3.3 and 3.4 is the specification of non-spatial and spatial structure and behavior of each type of agent in traffic jam management interaction scenario.

Figure 3.13 is the illustration of electricity replenishing interaction process. In this electricity replenishing interaction process, there are three agents: Electricity stations, control center and electric-taxis. The detail of process is described as below: In the beginning user execute the simulation (step1). Immediately, simulation initial and electricity stations, control center and electric-taxis (step2-2, 2-3 and 2-4), and simulation time is begin running and updating (step2-1). During the simulation period, electricity stations will update its' state (busy/idle) (step3). After generating and simulating for a while, electric-taxis can be divided into two kind of electric-taxis: Some electric-taxis are in replenishing and others are still in operation with electricity shortage (represented by the longest transverse thick-line). Electric-taxis those are in operation with electricity shortage ask electricity shortage information to control center and other electric-taxis those are in replenishing (step4-1 and 4-2). The electric-taxis that are in replenishing and control center to other electric-taxis those are in operation (step5-1 and 5-2).

| Agent | Duty / Goal | Non-spatial behavior | Non-spatial structure | |
| --- | --- | --- | --- | --- |
| | | | Variables | Functions |
| Electric-taxis A (moving freely) | 1. Avoid the traffic jam | 1. Receive the information from other taxis that getting in the traffic jam | 1. Record road condition | 1. Setting color function() |
| | | | | 2. Setting Id function() |
| | 2. Animation | 2. Find another shortest path that excluded the road which is under the traffic jam and move on | 2. Id | 3. Perceive function() |
| | | | | 4. Action function() |
| | | | | 5. Update the road condition function() |
| | | | 3. Color | 6. Shortest path selection function() |
| Electric-taxis B (get in traffic jam) | 1. Inform other taxis to avoid the traffic jam | 1. Updating the road information and send to other taxis. | 1. Record road condition | 1. Setting color function() |
| | | | | 2. Setting Id function() |
| | | | | 3. perceive function() |
| | 2. Animation | | 2. Id | 4. Action function() |
| | | | 3. Color | 5. Update the road condition function() |

**Table 3.3:** The specification of non-spatial structure and behavior of each type of agent in traffic jam management interaction scenario.

| Agent | Duty / Goal | Spatial behavior | Spatial structure | |
|---|---|---|---|---|
| | | | Variables | Functions |
| Electric-taxis A (moving freely) | 1. Avoid the traffic jam | 1. Moving on the road which is not getting in the traffic jam | 1. x coordinate | 1. Setting taxi location function() |
| | 2. Animation | | 2. y coordinate | 2. Setting taxi velocity function() |
| | | | 3. x velocity | 3. Stop taxi function() |
| | | | 4. y velocity | 4. Modified taxi velocity function() |
| Electric-taxis B (get in traffic jam) | 1. Inform other taxis to avoid the traffic jam | 1. Moving on the road which is getting in the traffic jam | 1. x coordinate | 1. Setting taxi location function() |
| | | | 2. y coordinate | 2. Setting taxi velocity function() |
| | 2. Animation | | 3. x velocity | 3. Stop taxi function() |
| | | | 4. y velocity | 4. Modified taxi velocity function() |

**Table 3.4:** The specification of spatial structure and behavior of each type of agent in traffic jam management interaction scenario.

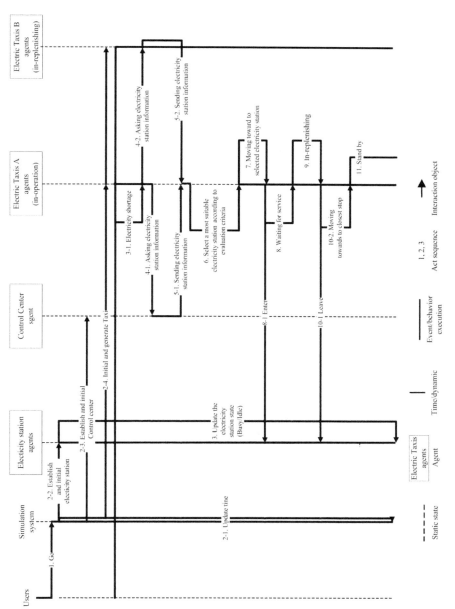

**Figure 3.13:** Electricity replenishing interaction process.

And then electric-taxis those are in lack of electricity select a most suitable electricity station according evaluation criteria (step6). After, electric-taxi moves to selected elected station (step7). When electric-taxis enter in or leave the selected electricity station, the electricity station will update its' state (busy/idle) (step8-1 and 10-1). When electric-taxi arrives at electricity station, driver has to waiting for replenishing until there are no cars in front of him (step8-2 and 9). Finally, after replenishing finished, electric-taxi will move to the closest stop and stand by for assignment (step10-2).

Table 3.5 and 3.6 is the specification of non-spatial and spatial structure and behavior of each type of agent in the electricity replenishing interaction scenario.

| Duty / Goal | Spatial behavior | Spatial structure | |
| --- | --- | --- | --- |
| | | Variables | Functions |
| 1. Support electric-taxis to replenishing and come back quickly | 1. Sending the related stop and electric station information to electric-taxi A | 1. Color | 1. Setting color function() |
| | | | 2. Setting Electric station database function() |
| | | | 3. Setting Stop database function() |
| | | | 4. Perceive function() |
| | | | 5. Action function() |
| | | 2. Electric station database | 6. Information process function() |
| 2. Animation | | 3. Stop database | 7. Update electric-taxi function() |

**Table 3.5A:** The specification of non-spatial structure and behavior of Control Center in the electricity replenishing interaction scenario.

| Duty / Goal | Spatial behavior | Spatial structure | |
| --- | --- | --- | --- |
| | | **Variables** | **Functions** |
| 1. Replenish electricity and come back with the fastest speed | 1. Asking for the related stop and electric station information to control center and electric-taxi B | 1. Id | 1. Setting Id function()<br>2. Setting Color function()<br>3. Setting Electric station database function() |
| | | 2. Color | 4. Setting Stop database function() |
| | | 3. Electricity state | 5. Update electricity station function() |
| | | 4. Whether lack of electricity or not | 6. Update electricity state function() |
| | 2. Receiving the related stop and electric station information form control center and electric-taxi B | 5. Electricity station database | 7. Perceive function() |
| | 3. Select the most suitable electricity station according to selection mechanism | 6. Stop database | 8. Action function() |
| 2. Animation | 4. Select the closest stop according to selection mechanism | 7. Closest stop | 9. Update electricity station database function() |
| | | 8. Best electricity station | 10. Electricity station selection function()<br>11. The closest stop selection function() |

**Table 3.5B:** The specification of non-spatial structure and behavior of Electric-taxi A (in operation) in the electricity replenishing interaction scenario.

| Duty / Goal | Spatial behavior | Spatial structure | |
| --- | --- | --- | --- |
| | | Variables | Functions |
| 1. Provide the electric station information to other electric-taxis to avoid longer waiting time | 1. Sending the related electric station information to other electric-taxis | 1. Id | 1. Setting Id function() |
| | | | 2. Setting Color function() |
| | | | 3. Setting Electric station database function() |
| | | | 4. Update electricity state function() |
| | | 2. Color | 5. Update electricity station function() |
| | | 3. Electricity state | 6. Perceive function() |
| 2. Animation | 2. Replenishing | 4. Whether electricity is full or not | 7. Action function() |
| | 3. Whether electricity is full or not | 5. Electricity station database | |

**Table 3.5C:** The specification of non-spatial structure and behavior of Electric-taxi B (in replenishing) in the electricity replenishing interaction scenario.

| Duty / Goal | Spatial behavior | Spatial structure | |
|---|---|---|---|
| | | Variables | Functions |
| 1. Service for the vehicle which is lack of electricity | 1. Replenishing for the vehicle which is lack of electricity | 1. Id | 1. Setting Id function() |
| | | 2. Color | 2. Setting Color function() |
| | | | 3. Update electricity station state function() |
| 2. Animation | 2. Waiting for the vehicle which needs to replenishing electricity | 3. Electricity station state | 4. Perceive function() |
| | | 4. Capacity | 5. Action function() |

**Table 3.5D:** The specification of non-spatial structure and behavior of Electric station in the electricity replenishing interaction scenario.

| Duty / Goal | Spatial behavior | Spatial structure | |
|---|---|---|---|
| | | Variables | Functions |
| 1. Support electric-taxis to replenishing and come back quickly | | 1 .x coordinate | 1. Setting x_y position function() |
| 2. Animation | | 2. y coordinate | |

**Table 3.6A:** The specification of spatial structure and behavior of Control Center in the electricity replenishing interaction scenario.

| Duty / Goal | Spatial behavior | Spatial structure | |
|---|---|---|---|
| | | Variables | Functions |
| 1. Replenishing electricity and come back with the fastest speed | 1. Move to the most suitable electricity station | 1. x coordinate | 1. Setting electric-taxi location function() |
| | | 2. y coordinate | 2. Setting electric-taxi velocity function() |
| | | 3. x velocity | 3. Stop electric-taxi function() |
| 2. Animation | 2. Move to the closest stop | 4. y velocity | 4. Modified electric-taxi velocity function() |

**Table 3.6B:** The specification of spatial structure and behavior of Electric-taxi A (in operation) in the electricity replenishing interaction scenario.

| Duty / Goal | Spatial behavior | Spatial structure | |
|---|---|---|---|
| | | Variables | Functions |
| 1. Provide the electric station information to other electric-taxis to avoid longer waiting time | | 1. x coordinate | 1. Setting electric-taxi location function() |
| | | 2. y coordinate | 2. Setting electric-taxi velocity function() |
| 2. Animation | | 3. x velocity | 3. Stop electric-taxi function() |
| | | 4. y velocity | 4. Modified electric-taxi velocity function() |

**Table 3.6C:** The specification of spatial structure and behavior of Electric-taxi B (in replenishing) in the electricity replenishing interaction scenario.

| Duty / Goal | Spatial behavior | Spatial structure | |
|---|---|---|---|
| | | Variables | functions |
| 1. Service for the vehicle which is lack of electricity | | 1. x coordinate | 1. Setting x_y position function() |
| 2. Animation | | 2. y coordinate | |

**Table 3.6D:** The specification of spatial structure and behavior of Electric station in the electricity replenishing interaction scenario

### 3.3.4    The Specification of Mechanisms and Algorithms used in the Electric-taxi DAR Operation System

In this sub-section, we will specify the all of the mechanisms and algorithms that used in the electric-taxi DAR operation system. All of the mechanisms and algorithms will be categorized to three part: (1) Incident management. (traffic jam). (2) Electric-taxi dial-a-ride management. (3) Replenishing electricity mechanism. The detail of all of the mechanisms and algorithms are described as follow:

1.  Incident management (traffic jam)

    i.   **The mechanism of identifying the traffic jam**: If an electric-taxi get in a road and its' speed slow down, we call the state of the electric-taxi is getting in traffic jam.

    ii.  **The mechanism of avoiding the traffic jam**: When a electric-taxi gets in the traffic jam, the electric-taxi will send the related traffic jam information (for example: Which road is under traffic jam) to every electric-taxi. If other electric-taxis are going to enter this road, they will switch into other paths based on the shortest path selection mechanism that excludes the road which is under traffic jam.

2.  Electric-taxi dial-a-ride management problem

    i.   **How to choose the proper car to pick passenger up and deliver**: There are eight stops in our system. Every electric-taxi has to stand by in the stop, so control center choose the electric-taxi which is idle and the distance from the electric-taxi to specific passenger is the shortest. The calculation of distance between electric-taxi and passenger is just calculated based on the distance of the straight line that from electric-taxi location to passenger location.

ii. **How to choose the passenger which you want to pick-up / service**: FIFO (first in first out). That means when passengers appear in the system, control center will pick the passenger who is first appears in the system to service. Then control center will chose the second one and so on.

iii. **What is the next step to driver, after driver delivering passenger to his/her destination**: Stand by and check whether electric-taxi needs to be replenished or not.

iv. **How to choose the pathway to deliver passenger to his/her destination**: Search the shortest path by algorithm.

3. Replenishing electricity mechanism

   i. **How to schedule electric-taxis whom are waiting for replenishing**: Apply FIFO (first in first out). That means the electric-taxi which is first enter in electric station, he should be served first.

   ii. **When a electric-taxi should be replenished**: According to literature review. When the electricity level less than 3.8kwh, the electric-taxi should be replenished. The default is 3.8.

   iii. **How long should an electric-taxi replenish electricity**: According to literature review. The default is 2 unit time (virtual unit time).

   iv. **How to select a proper electric station**: The electric station which is the closest station and its' waiting number less than 4 unit. If the closest station is too busy, we will choose another one which is closer and its' waiting number less than 4 unit. "The closest station" means the distance of straight line between electric-taxi and electric station is the shortest.

   v. **After finishing the replenishment, what is the next step to driver**: Go back to the closest stop and stand by. "The closest stop" means the distance of straight line between electric-taxi and stop is the shortest.

vi. **Where should we set up the electric station**: In our system, we apply random generation method to set up electric station randomly. The default of electric station is eight.

### 3.3.5    The Shortest Distance Problem Part 1: The Description of Dijkstra's Algorithm

Following, we specially illustrate the algorithm that we use to solve the shortest path problem. First, we describe the signs and their definition of Dijkstra's algorithm, the detail is described as Table 3.7. Next, we describe the procedure of Dijkstra's algorithm. Finally, we use an example to help understand the procedure of Dijkstra's algorithm.

| Sign | Definition |
|------|------------|
| s | Passenger start node |
| e | Passenger end node |
| N | Total node number |
| Dsj | The distance from start node to node j. $j = 1 \sim N$. $Dsj \geq 0$ (if start node doesn't connect with node j, then $Dsj = 0$) |
| SDj | The shortest distances that from start node to node j. $j=1 \sim N$, $SDj \geq 0$ (if start node equals to node j, then $SDj = 0$) |
| Cj | Whether the node j be chosen or not. $j=1 \sim N$. If Chosen, $Cj =1$, Otherwise, $Cj =0$ |
| PNj | The pre-node of node j, $j=1 \sim N$, $PNj = 1 \sim N$ |
| PSN | Pre-start node of node j, $j=1 \sim N$, $PSNj = 1 \sim N$ |
| CD | The current shortest distance |
| CN | The node of current shortest distance |

**Table 3.7:** The signs and their definition of Dijkstra's algorithm.

Following is the procedure of Dijkstra's algorithm. We divide the procedure of Dijkstra's algorithm into four steps. Step 1 is to find out the all of the distance that from start node to each node. Step 2 is to find out the current shortest distance node which will be the start node and the current start node will be the pre-node in the next loop. Step 3 and step 4 is to do the procedure as same as step 1 and step 2. And then program will repeats step 3 and step 4 until the loop stops. The only one difference between them is that the step 1 and step 2 run in the beginning of program. In the second loop, if we want to find out the distance that from start node to each node, we have to modify the step 1 and step 2 into step3 and step 4. When the loop finished, we can obtained the shortest path. The detail of each step is described as below.

```
// Step 1
If (Dsj != 0 || s == j), then SDj = Dsj;
Else, SDj = ∞;
//Step 2
For (int j=1; j<=N; j++){
   If (SDj < CD) then, CD = SDj;
   CN = j;
   PSN = s;
}
C_CN = 1;
For (int k=1; k<N; k++){
   //Step 3
   s = CN;
   For (int j=1; j<N; j++){
      If (Dsj + SD_s < SD_j) then SD_j = Dsj + SD_s; PNj = s;
   }
   //Step 4
   For (int j=1; j<=N; j++){
      If (SDj < CD && C_j == 0) then {
         CD = SDj;
         CN = j;
         PSN = s;
      }
   }
   C_CN = 1;
}
```

### 3.3.6    The Shortest Distance Problem Part 2: The Procedure Description of Dijkstra's Algorithm with Example

The shortest distance problem means how to find out the shortest distance from the start point to the end point. For example, in Figure 3.14, finding out the shortest distance from node S to node T is the shortest distance problem. The detail of solving the shortest distance problem is described as follows.

#### A. Find the Shortest Path

For solving the shortest path problem, the Dijkstra's algorithm is in common use. The objective of this algorithm is to find out the shortest path from S to T. The important attribute of this algorithm is that we can find out the shortest path that from start point to each point during the solving. Figure 3.14 is the example of the shortest path problem.

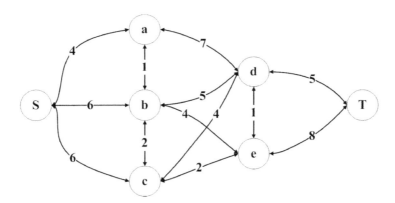

Figure 3.14: Example of the shortest path problem.

#### B. Important Concept

This algorithm divides all of the nodes into three parts.

1.  **Permanent sign set P** ( each sign represents the shortest distance form initial node to specific node in the network).

2.  **Temporal sign set T** (each sign represents the shortest distance from the initial node to the specific node that passes through the nodes of the set P).

3.  **Unsigned set U** ( the node is neither included in set P nor in set T).

## C. Illustration of Example

In Figure 3.15, P = {S, a, b}; [ ] represents permanent sign. The sign of node "b" is 5 that represents the shortest distance from "S" to "b" is 5. T = {c, d, e}; {} represents temporal sign. The sign of node "e" is 9 that represents the shortest distance from "S" of set P to "e" is 9. The path is S→a→b→e, {S, a, b} are all in set P. The sign of node "d" is 10 that represents the shortest distance from "S" of set P to "d" is 10. The path is S→a→b→d, {S, a, b} are all in the set P. U = {T}, that represents unsigned set.

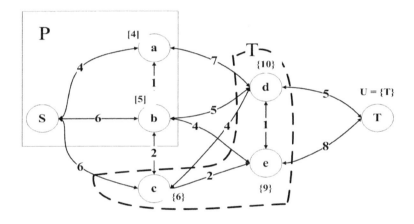

**Figure 3.15:** Illustration of example.

In Figure 3.16, P = {S}; the permanent sign of node "S" is 0. Include the neighbor node of node "S" to the temporal sign of set T. T = {a, b, c}, U = {d, e, T} are the unsigned set. The shortest node among the set T is node "a", the value of node "a" is 4. That represents the shortest distance from S to "a" is 4 (the distance from other nodes to node a are longer).

In Figure 3.17, we need to do some modification. Modification: P = {S, a}, T = {b, c, d}. Because "d" connects to "a", set T includes node "d". The temporal sign of set T must be modified: The sign of node b is Min {6, 4+1} = 5, so the sign of node b is changed into 5. Because node "c" doesn't connect to node "a", the sign of node c is also 6. For node "d", the temporal sign of node d is 4 + 7 = 11. Among the set T, the temporal sign of node b is the smallest that represents the shortest distance from S to b is 5. So set P includes node b.

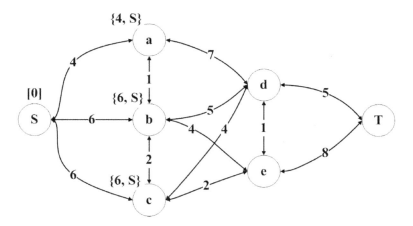

**Figure 3.16:** Step1 of solving example.

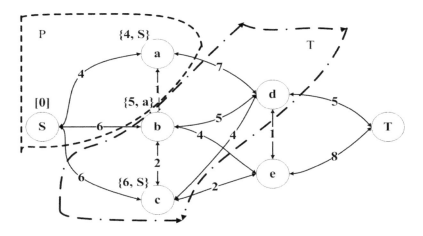

**Figure 3.17:** Step2 of solving example.

In Figure 3.18, we need to do some modification. Modification: P = {S, a, b}, T = {c, d, e}. Because "e" connects to "b", set T includes node "b". The temporal sign of set T must be modified: The sign of node c is Min {6, 6+2} = 6, so the temporal sign of node b is also the same. The sign of node d is Min {11, 5+5} = 10, so the sign of node d is changed to 10. So the temporal sign of node e is also 5 + 4 = 9. Among the set T, the temporal sign of node c is the smallest that represents the shortest distance from S to c is 6. So set P includes node c.

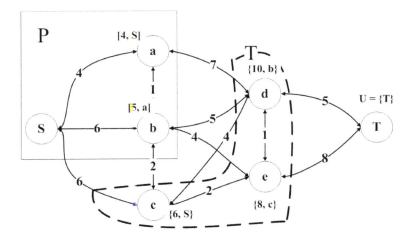

**Figure 3.18:** Step3 of solving example.

In Figure 3.19, we need to do some modification. Modification: P = {S, a, b, c}, T = {d, e}. Set T doesn't include any node. The temporal sign of set T must be modified: The sign of node d is Min {10, 6+4} = 10, so the temporal sign of node b is also the same. The sign of node e is Min {9, 6+2} = 8, so the sign of node e is changed to 8. Among the set T, the temporal sign of node e is the smallest that represents the shortest distance from S to e is 8. So set P includes node e.

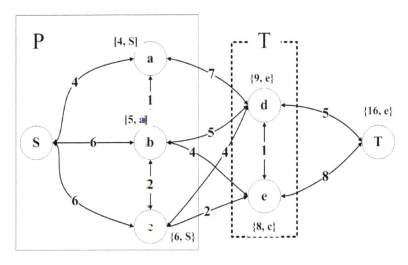

**Figure 3.19:** Step4 of solving example.

In Figure 3.20, we need to do some modification. Modification: P = {S, a, b, c, e}, T = {d, T}. Because "t" connects to "e", set T includes node "T". The temporal sign of set T must be modified: The sign of node d is Min {10, 8+1} = 9, so the temporal sign of node d is changed to 9. The sign of node T is 8 + 8 = 16. Among the set T, the temporal sign of node d is the smallest that represents the shortest distance from S to d is 9. So set P includes node d.

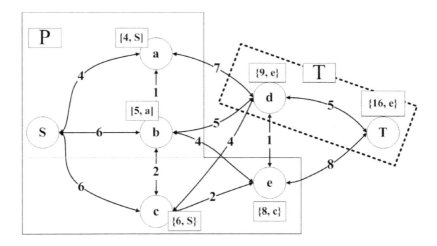

**Figure 3.20:** Step5 of solving example.

In Figure 3.21, we need to do some modification. Modification: P = {S, a, b, c, e, d}, T = {T}. The temporal sign of set T must be modified: The sign of node T is Min {16, 9+5} = 14, so the temporal sign of node T is changed to 14. There are no other nodes need to solve, so set P includes node T. And we finish the shortest path problem by applying Dijkstra's algorithm. The Figure 3.22 and Table 3.8 show the shortest path tree. The pre-point means the previous point of node of first row (for example: The pre-point of node "e" is node "c", so the process sequence is c→e not e→c).

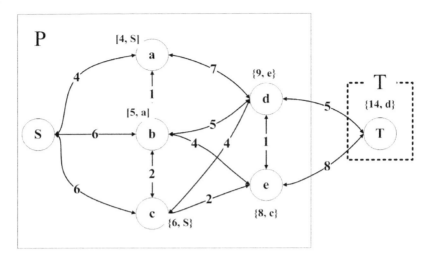

**Figure 3.21:** Step6 of solving example.

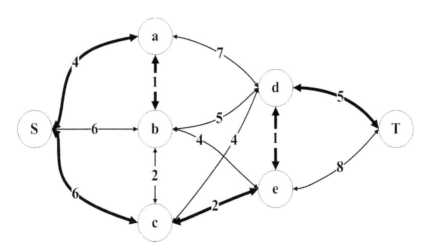

**Figure 3.22:** The shortest path of example.

|          | S     | a     | b     | c     | d     | e     | T     |
|----------|-------|-------|-------|-------|-------|-------|-------|
| S        | <u>0</u> | 4     | 6     | 6     | ∞     | ∞     | ∞     |
| a        |       | <u>4</u> | 5     | 6     | 11    | ∞     | ∞     |
| b        |       |       | <u>5</u> | 6     | 10    | 9     | ∞     |
| c        |       |       |       | <u>6</u> | 10    | 8     | ∞     |
| e        |       |       |       |       | 9     | <u>8</u> | 16    |
| d        |       |       |       |       | <u>9</u> |       | 14    |
| T        |       |       |       |       |       |       | <u>14</u> |
| Pre-node |       | <u>S</u> | <u>a</u> | <u>S</u> | <u>e</u> | <u>c</u> | <u>d</u> |

**Table 3.8:** The shortest path tree is described by table.

## 3.4    Select the Simulation Platform and Program Language

We use Anylogic 7 version as our simulation platform. XJ Technologies is a leading provider of dynamic simulation tools, technologies and consulting services for business applications. XJ Technologies designs, develops and markets AnyLogic - the first and only tool that brings together System Dynamics, Process-centric (Discrete Event), and Agent Based methods within one modeling language and one model development environment. AnyLogic was first shown at Winter Simulation Conference in year 2000. AnyLogic is the choice of thousands users worldwide, hundreds of commercial and governmental organizations and hundreds of universities. AnyLogic has become a corporate standard for simulation in many global companies.

In our simulation, we use java language as our program language. Java is an object-oriented program language. That makes modeling of agent-based simulation become easier. And its' flexibility makes it can operate in many different platforms (for example: linux, unix, Mac, Microsoft windows and so on). That's also its' the biggest advantage. On the other hand, AnyLogic is a java-based simulation platform, it just match our need. So we chose Anylogic as our simulation platform.

## 3.5    Creation and Simulation of Electric-taxi DAR Operation System

### 3.5.1    Creation of Electric-taxi DAR Operation System

In our simulation, we use java language as our program language. On the other hand, AnyLogic is a java-based simulation platform, it just match our need. So we chose Anylogic as our simulation platform.

According to the framework that proposed in the Section 2 and 3, we have constructed the multi-agent electric-taxi DAR operation system (Figure 3.24). Figure 3.23(a) to 3.23(c) are the decomposition of the multi-agent electric-taxi DAR operation system. Figure 3.23(a) illustrates the attributes of agent. The attributes of agent are extracted from the framework of agent. Figure 3.23(b) illustrates the states/behaviors of agent. The behaviors of agent are extracted from combining the framework of agent and interaction process. Figure 3.23(c) illustrates the management policies of electric-taxi DAR operation system. The management policies are completed by specific definition in the Section 3.

### 3.5.2    Simulation of Electric-taxi DAR Operation System and Setting

In this sub-section, we list the environment specification and simulation settings in the Table 3.9 and Table 3.10. The Figure 3.25 is the simulation of electric-taxi DAR operation system.

In computer environment, we use Microsoft Windows 7 Professional version 2014 Service pack 3 as our operation system. The CPU computer is Intel(R) Core(TM)2 6320 @ 1.86GHz and the RAM computer is 1.87Ghz, 0.99GB. The AnyLogic version is Anylogic 7 and the java version is JDK6.0.

In simulation settings, the number of taxi is 10. The number of stop and road is 8 and 18, respectively. And stop generation belongs to random generation. Other detail information is listed in Table 3.10.

## 3.6    Management Policies Establishment

In this sub-section, we specify each of management policies that used in the simulation. We establish three kinds of management policies. The first management policy is moving basis. The second management policy is

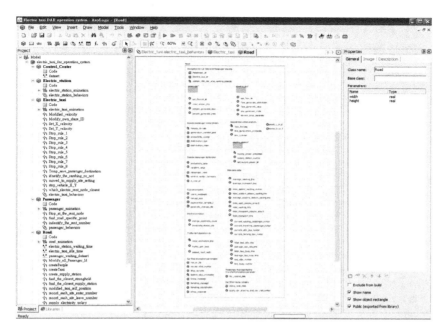

**Figure 3.23(a):** The agent attributes of electric-taxi.

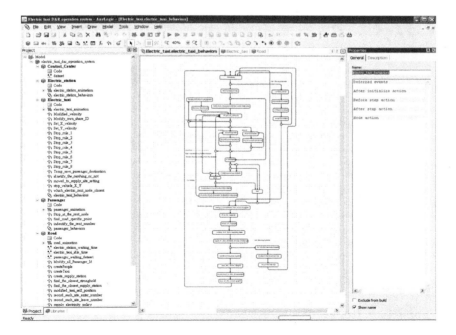

**Figure 3.23(b):** the agent state of electric-taxi DAR operation system operation system

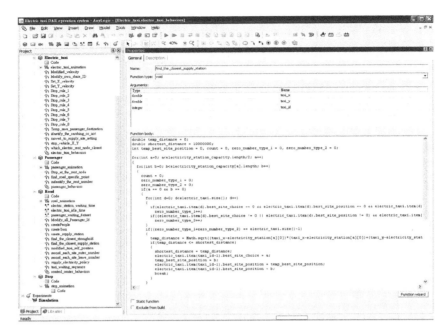

**Figure 3.23(c):** The management policies.

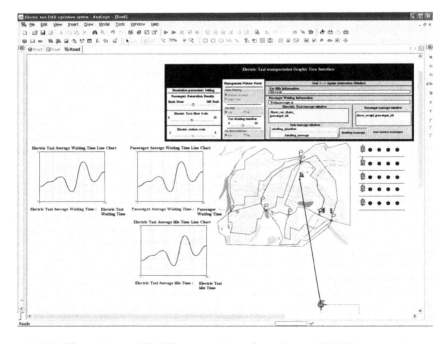

**Figure 3.24:** Electric-taxi DAR operation electric-taxi DAR operation system simulation system

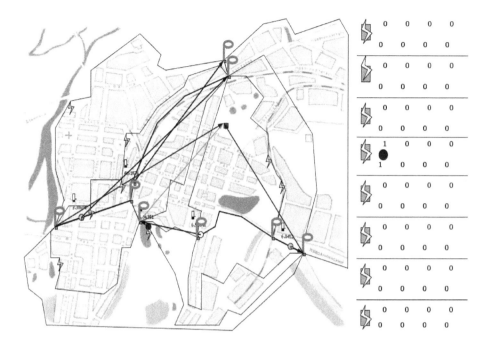

**Figure 3.25:** The simulation of electric-taxi DAR operation system

| Operation system | CPU | Ram | Anylogic version | Java version |
|---|---|---|---|---|
| Microsoft Windows 7 Professional version 2014 Service pack 3 | Intel(R) Core(TM)2 6320 @ 1.86GHz | 1.87Ghz, 0.99GB | Anylogic 7 | JDK 6.0 |

**Table 3.9:** Environment specification.

| Time accuracy | Stop at time | Simulation speed | Model time units per second | The number of taxi | The generation rate of passenger |
|---|---|---|---|---|---|
| 0.01 | 30 units | Virtual mode | 100 units | 10 | Normal (0.2) |

**Table 3.10:** Simulation settings in Anylogic 5.1 version

service area. The third management policy is car-sharing. Then we use these three kinds of management policies to construct simulation scenes and observe the result of simulation. The simulation scenario will be described in the Chapter 4. The Figure 3.26 shows the management policies framework and relationship with simulation scenes. The detail of each of management policies will be specified in the 3.5.1~3.5.3 sub-sections.

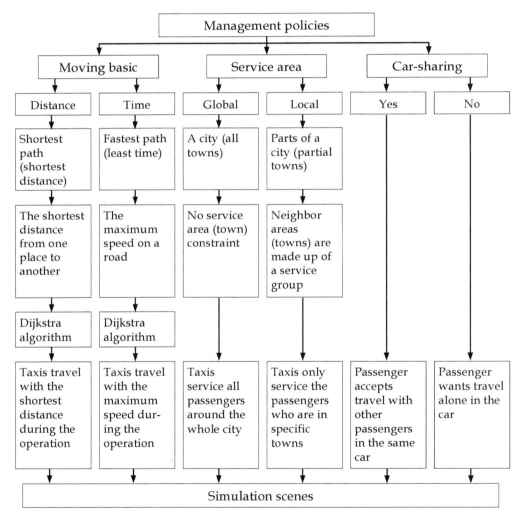

**Figure 3.26:** Management Policies.

### 3.6.1 Paths Planning

Moving basis is divided into two types: Distance and time. This management policy means the moving of electric taxi is based on distance or time. Distance management policy represents the moving of electric taxi is based on shortest distance from starting point to destination, so the total traveling distance is the shortest. On the other hand, time management policy represents the moving of electric taxi is based on least time from starting point to destination, so the total traveling time is the least. For shortest distance problem, the solution is applying the Dijkstra's algorithm. The detail of Dijkstra's algorithm is specified in the sub-section 3.5.2. For least time problem, the solution is the same as the shortest distance problem. The chosen basis of least time path is according to the maximum speed (MS) on a specific road (Taiwan Area National Freeway bureau. 2009). But we modify the chosen basis to be more suitable for our simulation. However, we do not only consider how fast an electric taxi moves on a road; we more care about how fast an electric taxi finishes a road. So we divide the road length by MS to obtain the finish time. And we regard finish time as the chosen basis of least time path, we call it least finish time (LFT).

Figure 3.27 is a simple shortest and fastest path problem. Through the specification of this shortest fastest path problem, we can clearly understand our moving basis management policy. The black number on the arc represents the distance between two nodes, so the distance from starting node to middle node is 20 meters. The blue number on the arc represents the MS on the road, so the MS on the road A is 100meters / 1second.

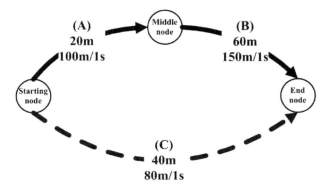

**Figure 3.27:** Shortest and fastest path problem.

For the shortest path problem form starting node to end node, there are two paths. One is starting node→A→B→end node (20m + 60m = 80m) and the other is starting node→C→end node (only 40m), so through the Dijkstra's algorithm, the shortest path is road C (40meters). For fastest path problem (according to the MS on a specific road), because the MS of road A, B and C are 100m/1s, 150m/1s and 80m/1s respectively. Obviously, the MS of road A and B are higher than road C, so through the Dijkstra's algorithm, the fastest path is starting node→A→B→end node. For the same fastest path problem, we use LFT to be the chosen basis. We calculate the LFT of road A (20m/(100m/1s)), B(60m/(150m/1s)) and C(40m/(80m /1s)) respectively. We can obtain the LFT of road A, B and C is 0.2s, 0.4s and 0.5s. And through the Dijkstra's algorithm, the fastest path starting node→A→B→end node is 0.2s + 0.4s = 0.6s, the other path starting node→C→end node is 0.5s. So the real fastest path is starting node→C→end node. So we use the MS be the chosen basis of the fastest problem can obtain a wrong and irrational solution. Evidently, our LFT chosen basis is more accurate and rational than MS.

### 3.6.2    Service Area

Service area is divided into two types: global and local. Global service area represents each electric taxi can serve all of the passengers around a city. Local service area represents each electric taxi has its' own service area, just parts of city. In the electric taxi DAR operation system simulation, we set eight points (are equal to towns), passengers will appear from these points (towns). When we chose global service area management policy, we permit each of electric taxis deliver and pick up any passenger. So each of electric taxis can serve the passengers of each of eight points (towns). When we chose local service area management policy, we restrict the service area of every electric taxi. We divide eight points (towns) into three groups. The division basis is grouping neighbor points (towns) into together. So there are three service groups for electric taxis. Figure 3.28 shows the eight points and local service area groups. Group A is composed of three rhombuses, group B is consisted of two rectangles and group C is made up of three circles. Local service type 1: electric taxis serve the passengers who want to travel from group B to group A or move inside the group B. Local service type 2: electric taxis serve the passengers

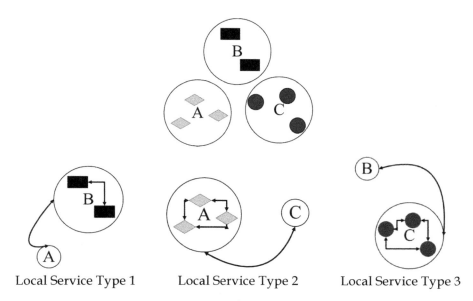

Local Service Type 1        Local Service Type 2        Local Service Type 3

**Figure 3.28:** Service area and local service area groups.

who want to travel from group A to group C or move inside the group A. Local service type 3: electric taxis serve the passengers who want to travel from group C to group B or move inside the group C.

### 3.6.3    Car-Pool

Car-pool management policy admits passengers decide whether they can travel with other passengers in the same car by themselves through the interaction of passengers and electric taxi drivers. Following, we describe the car-pool procedure. First, control center will assign a passenger to an electric taxi. Meanwhile, control center will ask the car-pool will of passenger. If the answer of passenger is "not", electric taxi will only pick-up and deliver one passenger until the task is finished. If the answer of passenger is "yes" and the driver encounters other passengers during the traveling period, driver will ask other passengers whether they want to go together until there is no passenger in the car. This management policy can make the passenger number in the car is not only one anymore. This management policy can make the passengers who have different starting points or destinations take a travel together.

### 3.6.4    Car-Sharing

Car-sharing management policy admits passengers rent a car to drive toward their destinations. The difference between car-pool and car-sharing is that passengers don't need to wait for an electric taxi to pick them up in car-sharing; they can get a car in the closest site and drive by themselves, finally, they return the car in a site which is closest to their destinations and go to the terminals, decide whether they can travel with other passengers in the same car by themselves through the interaction of passengers and electric taxi drivers. Following, we describe the car-sharing procedure. First, control center will assign a passenger to an electric taxi. Meanwhile, control center will ask the car-pool will of passenger. If the answer of passenger is "not", electric taxi will only pick-up and deliver one passenger until the task is finished. If the answer of passenger is "yes" and the driver encounters other passengers during the traveling period, driver will ask other passengers whether they want to go together until there is no passenger in the car. This management policy can make the passenger number in the car is not only one anymore. This management policy can make the passengers who have different starting points or destinations take a travel together.

## 3.7    Graphic User Interface Construction

An available simulation model should be operated by user. Simulation model is not only established for animation. Simulation model should be verified and modified by user. A simulation model which can be operated by user will increase its application area and flexibility. For our electric taxi DAR operation system model, we construct three panels to make up a graphic user interface (GUI). The first panel is simulation parameter setting. This panel can provide user to set different passenger generation types and electric taxi amount. User can input the real data through collecting history records to make the simulation approach reality. The simulation parameters setting is diagramed as Figure 3.29.

The second panel is management policies panel. This panel can provide user to choose different management policies to study and observe the simulation results. Different management policy combinations will cause different simulation result. User can choose suitable management

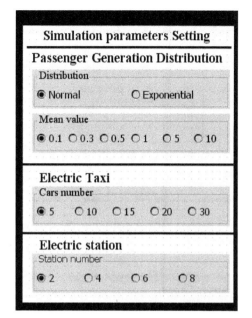

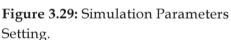

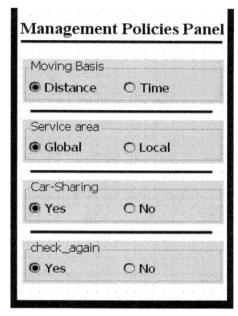

**Figure 3.29:** Simulation Parameters Setting.

**Figure 3.30:** Management Policies Panel.

policies to observe the simulation phenomena according to the realistic environment through this panel. The management policies panel is diagramed as Figure 3.30. All of the details of management policies are specified in the sub-section 3.5.

The third panel is diagramed as Figure 3.31. The third panel is user and agents interaction window. First, this panel provides the electric taxis idle and passengers waiting information to users. User can perceive the information which electric taxi is idle and which passenger is waiting for service immediately. And both of information is always up to date. In the Figure 3.28, No.9 electric taxi is idle and No.6, 10, 11, 12, 13 passengers are still waiting for service.

Second, this panel provides the interactive between user and electric taxis. In the animation, if an electric taxi deriver encounters a passenger who may be possible to go together electric taxi will stop and sending the message to the "electric taxi message window" (as Figure 3.31 User and Agents Interaction Procedure Step 1).

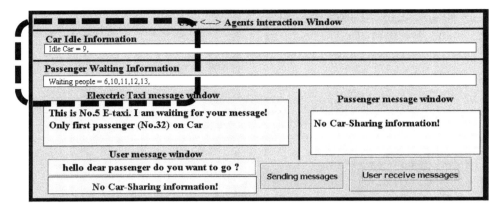

**Figure 3.31:** User and Agents Interaction Window.

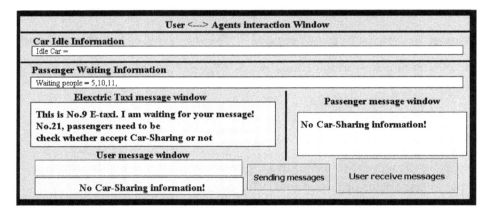

**Figure 3.32:** User and Agents Interaction Procedure Step 1.

The "electric taxi message window" shows "This is No.9 E-taxi. I am waiting for your message! No.21, passenger need to be check whether accept Car-sharing or not" message. After user perceiving this message, he can type a question to ask driver to negotiate with passenger (shows in Figure 3.33). In the Figure 3.33, user types the "hello dear passenger do you want to go?" message in the user message window. Then user presses the "sending message" button to send the message.

The negotiation message will show in the second frame of "user message window" and the negotiation result will show in the "passenger message window" (as Figure 3.34 User and Agents Interaction Procedure Step 3). The second frame of "user message window" shows "negotiation has finished!" message that represents driver has finished the communication with passenger. And the "passenger message window" shows "No.21 passenger is willing to go together!" message to inform user that passenger accepts the car-sharing traveling mechanism. When user accepts the message, he presses the "user receives message" button to inform the electric taxi driver that user has received the message. Then the electric taxi DAR operation system simulation will continue.

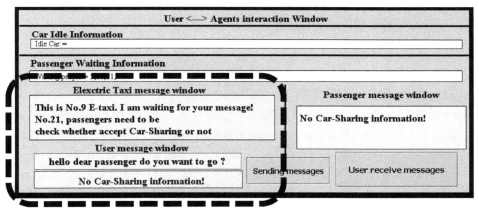

**Figure 3.33:** User and Agents Interaction Procedure Step 2.

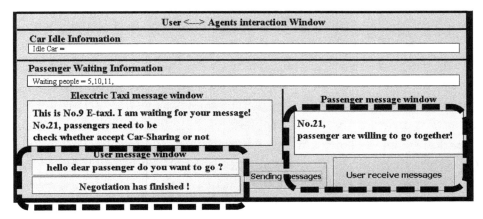

**Figure 3.34:** User and Agents Interaction Procedure Step 3.

# 4

# Case Study

## 4.1   Scenario Description

A city includes eight towns. There are total eighteen roads in the city. An electric taxi company has established in the city for many years. It has its' own electric taxi fleet. Each of towns has one electric taxi stop. The company has finite electric taxis, but it has to satisfy all of the passengers around the city. In this city, every passenger uses dial-a-ride (DAR) service mechanism to ask a taxi to serve them. On the other hand, because taxis are driven by electricity, they will run out of the taxis' electricity one day. Once taxis lack of electricity, they have to replenish the energy. So the company also has set up eight electric stations. But the company encounters a troublesome problem: their electric taxi company can't obtain a better performance (ex: lower passenger waiting time, higher revenue and so on). So the company wants to know how to manage the electric taxis system effectively. And there are two constraints: The first is the passenger amount is more over the electric taxi amount. The second is the electricity of each of taxis is also finite and when an electric taxi has to replenish its' energy, he can't serve any passenger during the replenishment period. Under this severe condition, the management of electric taxis is very important. In order to solve this problem, we construct an electric taxi DAR operation system to simulate the operation of the electric taxi system of the city. And we combine different management policies to add into the simulation system to observe the simulation result. Our performance measure is passenger average waiting time in the simulation system. Then we will collect and analyze the data obtained from simulation. Finally, the analysis results can be the suggestions for the electric taxi company.

### 4.1.1    Case 1

For an electric taxi company, it has its own electric taxi fleet. And it has eight electric station, no car-pool and car-sharing management policies. Now it wants to know what the most feasible scale of electric taxi is. Because it thinks: "If the electric taxi scale is too large, the passenger waiting time will be lower but most of the state of electric taxis will be idle during the rush hour. If the electric taxi scale is too small, the passenger waiting time will be higher but most of the state of electric taxis will be busy during the rush hour."

Under this condition, we simulate the rush hour in a metropolis by setting the passenger generation distribution belongs to normal distribution with mean value 0.3. For eight generation nodes, the generation rate of two specific nodes are double than other nodes. Under this setting, we simulate two nodes' passengers' demands are higher.

First, we want to find out how large the scale of electric taxi fleet is feasible. So we fix five parameters: 1. passenger distribution belongs to normal distribution with the mean value (0.3). 2. Electric station number is 6. 3. Paths planning: we choose the shortest path as our path planning. 4. Car-pool: so far, we do not accept car-pool. 5. Car-sharing: so far, we do not accept car-sharing. In order to find out what's the feasible scale of electric taxi fleet, we vary the electric taxi number from 5 to 20 to observe the variances of passenger average waiting time and electric taxi average idle time.

From Table 4.1, we know the mean value of passenger average waiting time is 0.072 (time unit) and electric taxi average idle time is 0.2997 (time unit). From Figure 4.1, we can obviously realize that if the scale of taxi idle time is less than 7, the passenger average waiting time is too high. Contrary, if the scale of taxi idle time is more than 7, the electric taxi average idle time is too high. The most important thing is what the most feasible scale of electric taxi fleet is. We decide the scale of electric taxi fleet is 11, for point 11, because both of the passenger average waiting time and electric taxi average idle time is below the mean value.

Second, after deciding the scale of electric taxi fleet, the company wants to know how large the scale of electric station is feasible. If the scale of electric station is too small, the electric taxi waiting time will be too long. So we fix four parameters: 1. passenger distribution belongs to normal distribution with the mean value (0.3). 2. Electric taxi fleet number is

| Electric taxi number | Passenger average waiting time | Electric taxi average idle time |
|:---:|:---:|:---:|
| 5 | 0.1370 | 0.0628 |
| 6 | 0.1319 | 0.0785 |
| 7 | 0.1093 | 0.1022 |
| 8 | 0.0825 | 0.1448 |
| 9 | 0.0792 | 0.2378 |
| 10 | 0.0785 | 0.2561 |
| 11 | 0.0642 | 0.2759 |
| 12 | 0.0632 | 0.3225 |
| 13 | 0.0596 | 0.3395 |
| 14 | 0.0577 | 0.3598 |
| 15 | 0.0542 | 0.3776 |
| 16 | 0.0516 | 0.4083 |
| 17 | 0.0496 | 0.4144 |
| 18 | 0.0459 | 0.4364 |
| 19 | 0.0449 | 0.4727 |
| 20 | 0.0433 | 0.4794 |
| Mean Value | 0.0720 | 0.2997 |

**Table 4.1:** Passenger average waiting time and Electric taxi average idle time.

11. 3. Paths planning: we choose the shortest path as our path planning. 4. Car-pool: so far, we do not accept car-pool. 5. Car-sharing: so far, we do not accept car-sharing. In order to find out what's the feasible scale of electric station, we vary the electric station number from 1 to 8 to observe the variances of passenger average waiting time and electric taxi average waiting time.

From Table 4.2, we know the mean value of passenger average waiting time is 0.0742 (time unit) and electric taxi average waiting time in queue is 0.0687 (time unit). From Figure 4.2, we can obviously realize that

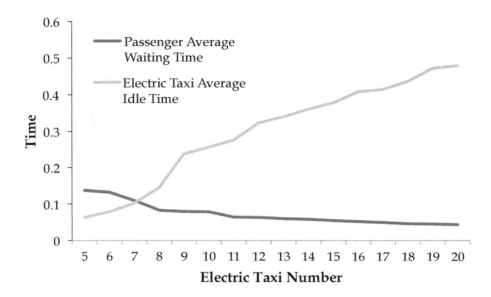

**Figure 4.1** Passenger average waiting time and Electric taxi average idle time.

if the scale of electric station increases, the passenger average waiting time and electric taxi waiting time will decrease. Contrary, if the scale of electric station decreases, the passenger average waiting time and electric taxi waiting time will increase. We find out that if the waiting time of an electric taxi in queue is longer, the passenger have to wait for a long time. When the waiting time of an electric taxi is long, the passenger satisfaction is low. From the scale of electric station is equal to or larger than 4, both of the passenger average waiting time and electric taxi average waiting time are below the mean value. And the most important thing is what the most feasible scale of electric station is. We find out that if the scale of electric taxi fleet is equal to or large than 5, the waiting time of an electric taxi begins converging. Hence, we decide the scale of electric station is 5.

Third, the company has decide the most feasible scale of electric taxi and electric station, following the company wants to know which paths planning is better or more suitable for its' electric taxi fleet and electric taxi company operation. So we fix five parameters: 1. passenger distribution belongs to normal distribution with the mean value (0.3). 2. Paths

| Electric station number | Passenger Average Waiting time | Electric Taxi Average Waiting Time |
|:---:|:---:|:---:|
| 1 | 0.1072 | 0.1294 |
| 2 | 0.0924 | 0.0964 |
| 3 | 0.0800 | 0.0732 |
| 4 | 0.0662 | 0.0579 |
| 5 | 0.0655 | 0.0507 |
| 6 | 0.0642 | 0.0492 |
| 7 | 0.0619 | 0.0465 |
| 8 | 0.0610 | 0.0443 |
| Mean value | 0.0742 | 0.0685 |

**Table 4.2:** Passenger average waiting time and Electric taxi average waiting time.

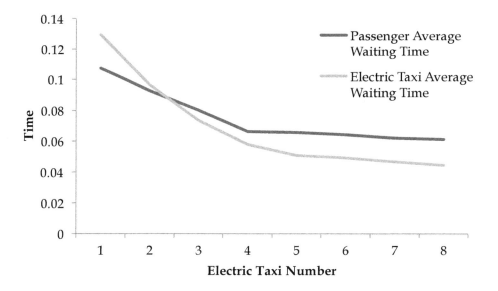

**Figure 4.2** Passenger average waiting time and Electric taxi average waiting time.

planning: we choose the least time as our path planning. 3. Electric station number is 5. 4. Car-pool: so far, we do not accept car-pool. 5. Car-sharing: so far, we do not accept car-sharing. In order to find out which paths planning is better; we vary the electric taxi number from 5 to 20 to observe the variances of passenger average waiting time and electric taxi average idle time.

From Table 4.3, we can find out the mean value of passenger average waiting time (0.0641) under least time path planning is better than shortest distance path planning (0.0720). And from number 11, all of the passenger average waiting time data is lower than mean value.

| Electric Taxi Number | Least Time | Shortest Distance |
|:---:|:---:|:---:|
| 5 | 0.1324 | 0.1370 |
| 6 | 0.1246 | 0.1319 |
| 7 | 0.0906 | 0.1093 |
| 8 | 0.0726 | 0.0825 |
| 9 | 0.0660 | 0.0792 |
| 10 | 0.0643 | 0.0785 |
| 11 | 0.0582 | 0.0642 |
| 12 | 0.0532 | 0.0632 |
| 13 | 0.0520 | 0.0596 |
| 14 | 0.0511 | 0.0577 |
| 15 | 0.0495 | 0.0542 |
| 16 | 0.0472 | 0.0516 |
| 17 | 0.0448 | 0.0496 |
| 18 | 0.0423 | 0.0459 |
| 19 | 0.0396 | 0.0449 |
| 20 | 0.0371 | 0.0433 |
| Mean Value | 0.0641 | 0.0720 |

**Table 4.3:** Passenger average waiting time.

From Figure 4.3, we can clearly know all of the passenger average waiting time is better under least time path planning. And there is a trend in Figure 4.3. First, if the scale of electric taxi fleet increases, the passenger average waiting time will decrease. Contrary, if the scale of electric taxi fleet decreases, the passenger average waiting time will increase. Second, we find out that if the scale of electric taxi fleet is equal to or large than 11, the passenger average waiting time begins converging. In brief, the company adds more electric taxi in the electric taxi fleet that only decreases small passenger average waiting time but increase more electric taxi idle time.

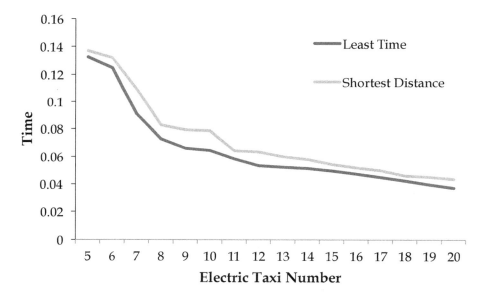

**Figure 4.3:** Passenger average waiting time line chart.

From Table 4.4, we can find out the mean value of electric taxi average idle time (0.2826) under least time path planning is better than shortest distance path planning (0.2997). And only the electric taxi number equals to or small than 11, all of the passenger average waiting time data is lower than mean value. From Table 4.4, we know the mean value of electric taxi average idle time is 0.2826 (time unit). In Figure 4.4, we can clearly know all of the electric taxi average idle time is better under least time path

| Electric Taxi Number | Least Time | Shortest Distance |
|:---:|:---:|:---:|
| 5 | 0.0501 | 0.0628 |
| 6 | 0.0523 | 0.0785 |
| 7 | 0.0695 | 0.1022 |
| 8 | 0.1399 | 0.1438 |
| 9 | 0.2220 | 0.2378 |
| 10 | 0.2528 | 0.2651 |
| 11 | 0.2713 | 0.2759 |
| 12 | 0.3056 | 0.3225 |
| 13 | 0.3310 | 0.3395 |
| 14 | 0.3391 | 0.3598 |
| 15 | 0.3552 | 0.3776 |
| 16 | 0.3861 | 0.4083 |
| 17 | 0.3880 | 0.4144 |
| 18 | 0.4245 | 0.4364 |
| 19 | 0.4513 | 0.4727 |
| 20 | 0.4836 | 0.4974 |
| Mean Value | 0.2826 | 0.2997 |

**Table 4.4:** Electric taxi average idle time.

planning. And there is a trend in Figure 4.4. First, if the scale of electric taxi fleet increases, the electric taxi average idle time will increase. Contrary, if the scale of electric taxi fleet decreases, the electric taxi average idle time will decrease. Second, we find out that if the scale of electric taxi fleet is equal to or less than 11, the electric taxi average idle time becomes lower than mean value. So we can make a brief summary: first, the electric taxi company applies least time as path planning is more suitable for electric taxi fleet and passengers. Second, only in point 11, the passenger average waiting time and electric taxi average idle time are lower than mean value. The result of data analysis is the same as the data analysis of most suitable electric taxi fleet that we describe before.

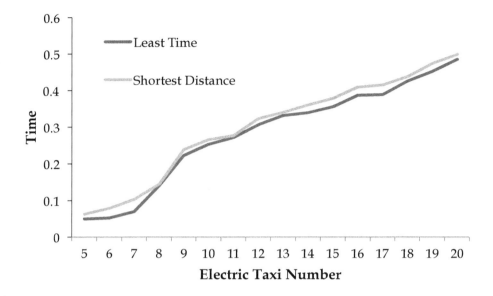

**Figure 4.4:** Electric taxi average idle time line chart.

### 4.1.2    Case 2

After electric taxi company decides the electric taxi fleet scale, electric station scale and path planning. Besides, the electric taxi company sets performance measures: passenger average waiting time and electric taxi average idle time. The standard of these two performance measures are the mean values which we describe before: 0.0641 and 0.2886 (time unit). Under this setting, the electric taxi company runs the electric taxi fleet for many months. So far, their company operation always can satisfy the standard of performance measures. However, they discover an interesting phenomenon: "some passengers' destinations are the same or on the same path". So the electric taxi company comes up with an interesting idea: "maybe we can let those passengers whose destinations are the same or on the same path take the same car." Therefore, the electric taxi company wants to add car-pool management policy into the electric taxi operation. Nevertheless, they want to know the performance of car-pool to measure the feasibility.

Hence we fix five parameters to do the simulation: 1. passenger distribution belongs to normal distribution with the mean value (0.3). 2. Paths planning: we choose the least time as our path planning. 3. Electric station number is 5. 4. Car-pool: we do apply car-pool. 5. Car-sharing: so far, we do not accept car-sharing. In order to find out whether apply car-pool is better or not; we vary the electric taxi number from 5 to 20 to observe the variances of passenger average waiting time and electric taxi average idle time.

From Table 4.5, we can find out the mean value of passenger average waiting time (0.0555) under Car-Pool is better than No Car-Pool (0.0641). And from number 9, all of the passenger average waiting time data is lower than mean value. So we can understand that if we apply car-pool in our electric taxi operation, we only need less cars but achieve the standard of performance measure.

| Electric Taxi Number | No Car-Pool | Car-Pool |
|---|---|---|
| 5 | 0.1424 | 0.0999 |
| 6 | 0.1246 | 0.0849 |
| 7 | 0.0906 | 0.0789 |
| 8 | 0.0726 | 0.0716 |
| 9 | 0.0660 | 0.0555 |
| 10 | 0.0643 | 0.0525 |
| 11 | 0.0582 | 0.0499 |
| 12 | 0.0532 | 0.0494 |
| 13 | 0.0520 | 0.0492 |
| 14 | 0.0511 | 0.0476 |
| 15 | 0.0495 | 0.0468 |
| 16 | 0.0472 | 0.0453 |
| 17 | 0.0448 | 0.0431 |
| 18 | 0.0423 | 0.0387 |
| 19 | 0.0396 | 0.0376 |
| 20 | 0.0371 | 0.0365 |
| Mean Value | 0.0641 | 0.0555 |

**Table 4.5:** Passenger average waiting time.

From Figure 4.5, we can clearly know all of the passenger average waiting time is lower under Car-Pool. And there is a trend in Figure 4.5. First, if the scale of electric taxi fleet increases, the passenger average waiting time will decrease. Contrary, if the scale of electric taxi fleet decreases, the passenger average waiting time will increase. Second, we find out that if the scale of electric taxi fleet is equal to or large than 11, the passenger average waiting time begins converging. In brief, the company adds more electric taxi in the electric taxi fleet that only decreases small passenger average waiting time but increase more electric taxi idle time. And the electric taxi company just needs the same electric taxi number; we can obtain the better result than before.

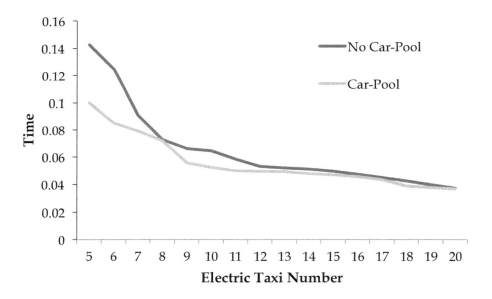

**Figure 4.5:** Passenger average waiting time line chart.

From Table 4.6, we can find out the mean value of electric taxi average idle time (0.2717) under Car-Pool is better than No Car-Pool (0.2826). And only the electric taxi number equals to or less than 11, all of the passenger average waiting time data is lower than mean value. And we realize that if we apply car-pool in our electric taxi operation, we only need less cars but achieve the good performance measure than own more cars.

| Electric Taxi Number | No Car-Pool | Car-Pool |
|:---:|:---:|:---:|
| 5 | 0.0501 | 0.0501 |
| 6 | 0.0523 | 0.0508 |
| 7 | 0.0695 | 0.0640 |
| 8 | 0.1399 | 0.1360 |
| 9 | 0.2220 | 0.2083 |
| 10 | 0.2528 | 0.2129 |
| 11 | 0.2713 | 0.2547 |
| 12 | 0.3056 | 0.2766 |
| 13 | 0.3310 | 0.3041 |
| 14 | 0.3391 | 0.3249 |
| 15 | 0.3552 | 0.3406 |
| 16 | 0.3861 | 0.3841 |
| 17 | 0.3880 | 0.3947 |
| 18 | 0.4245 | 0.4230 |
| 19 | 0.4513 | 0.4484 |
| 20 | 0.4836 | 0.4744 |
| Mean Value | 0.2826 | 0.2717 |

**Table 4.6:** Electric taxi average idle time.

From Table 4.6, we know the mean value of electric taxi average idle time is 0.2717 (time unit) under Car-Pool. In Figure 4.6, we can clearly know all of the electric taxi average idle time is better under Car-Pool. And there is a trend in Figure 4.6. First, if the scale of electric taxi fleet increases, the electric taxi average idle time will increase. Contrary, if the scale of electric taxi fleet decreases, the electric taxi average idle time will decrease. Second, we find out that if the scale of electric taxi fleet is equal to or less than 11, the electric taxi average idle time becomes lower than mean value. So we can make a brief summary: first, the electric taxi company applies least time as path planning is more suitable for electric taxi fleet and passengers. Second, from point 9 to point 11, the passenger average waiting

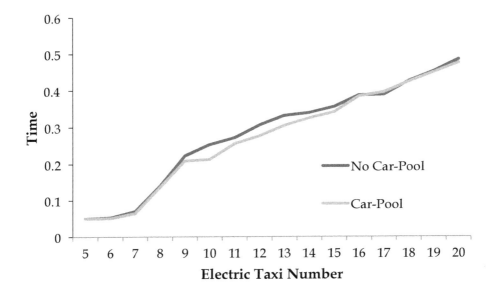

**Figure 4.6:** Electric taxi average idle time line chart.

time and electric taxi average idle time are lower than mean value. So we can make a conclusion for this discovery: the electric taxi company just need own 11, even 9 electric taxis, they can obtain the same or better the result of performance measure. After understand the data analysis, the electric taxi company is willing to practice the Car-Pool management policy in the electric taxi operation.

### 4.1.3    Case 3

So far, the electric taxi company satisfies its operation performance. But they still want to be more competitive. Hence they carefully inspect every detail. Finally, they observe a phenomenon: "around the downtown of a city, the population density is higher than other places. So the passenger number is also more than other areas." On the other hand, according to their investigation, almost 4 of 10 passengers must come from the downtown. And the passengers just want to go to neighborhood. But they discover two important points:

1.  Even though the distance form start point to destination is not so far

for taking an electric taxi, the fee is too expensive for passengers. So they won't to take an electric taxi.

2.    Although the passengers won't take an electric taxi, they also won't go to destination by walking.

Sum up the two points; we know that the electric taxi company has to provide a cheaper means of transportation. Therefore, the electric taxi company considers introducing a new management policy:"Car-Sharing". This management policy means the electric taxi company has to divide their electric taxi fleet into two types: 1. Normal electric taxi: an electric taxi which does anything we mentioned before. 2. Rental car: passengers only pay little fees to electric company, they can drive a car to any place where has the site of getting and return. Before applying car-sharing management policy, the electric taxi needs to consider three important things: 1. the rental car come from the original electric taxi fleet. So the scale of electric taxi fleet becomes smaller than before, the service level and efficiency may be debased. 2. Apply the car-sharing will get a better performance?

Hence we fix five parameters to do the simulation: 1. passenger distribution belongs to normal distribution with the mean value (0.3). 2. Paths planning: we choose the least time as our path planning. 3. Electric station number is 5. 4. Car-pool: we do apply car-pool. 5. Car-sharing: we do accept car-sharing. In order to find out whether apply car-sharing is better or not; we vary the electric taxi number from 5 to 20 to observe the variances of passenger average waiting time and electric taxi average idle time.

From Table 4.7, we can find out the mean value of passenger average waiting time (0.1014) under Car-Sharing is worse than No Car-Pool (0.0555). And we observe the data collected from simulation, under car-sharing, most of passenger average waiting time are worse, even double of No car-sharing. Hence, introducing car-sharing into the electric taxi operation can negatively affect the passenger waiting time.

From Figure 4.7, we can clearly know all of the passenger average waiting time is higher under Car-Sharing. And there is a trend in Figure 4.7. First, if the scale of electric taxi fleet increases, the passenger average waiting time will decrease. Contrary, if the scale of electric taxi fleet decreases, the passenger average waiting time will increase. Second, under no car-sharing, we find out that if the scale of electric taxi fleet is equal to

| Electric Taxi Number | No Car-Sharing | Car-Sharing |
|:---:|:---:|:---:|
| 5 | 0.0999 | 0.1555 |
| 6 | 0.0849 | 0.1314 |
| 7 | 0.0789 | 0.1286 |
| 8 | 0.0716 | 0.1202 |
| 9 | 0.0555 | 0.1169 |
| 10 | 0.0525 | 0.1148 |
| 11 | 0.0499 | 0.1002 |
| 12 | 0.0494 | 0.0991 |
| 13 | 0.0492 | 0.0971 |
| 14 | 0.0476 | 0.0945 |
| 15 | 0.0468 | 0.0942 |
| 16 | 0.0453 | 0.0898 |
| 17 | 0.0431 | 0.0891 |
| 18 | 0.0387 | 0.0779 |
| 19 | 0.0376 | 0.0546 |
| 20 | 0.0365 | 0.0411 |
| Mean Value | 0.0555 | 0.1003 |

**Table 4.7**: Passenger average waiting time.

or large than 11, the passenger average waiting time begins converging. In brief, the company adds more electric taxi in the electric taxi fleet that only decreases small passenger average waiting time but increase more electric taxi idle time. On the other hand, from Table 4.7 and Figure 4.7, we find out that divides the original electric taxi fleet into two types can decrease the service level of electric taxi fleet. In other words, due to the reduction of scale for electric taxi fleet, the electric taxi number of satisfying passenger demands also becomes less.

From Table 4.8, we can find out the mean value of electric taxi average idle time (0.2921) under Car-Sharing is also worse than No Car-Pool(0.2705). And only electric taxi number equals to or is less than 10

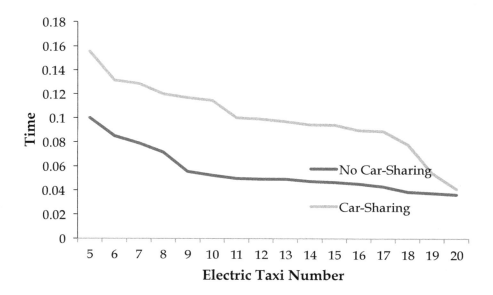

**Figure 4.7:** Passenger average waiting time line chart.

under Car-Sharing, the passenger average waiting time data is lower than mean value. And we realize that if we apply car-sharing in our electric taxi operation, we will get a worse electric taxi average idle time. That's an interesting phenomenon. We remain the same scale of total service car; we just divide the original electric taxi fleet into two types. But rental cars only serve two places. Other electric taxis serve the whole city. If one specific place doesn't appear any passenger for a long time (because the passenger generation belongs to normal distribution), the rental cars will still wait until a passenger appears. We can image that there are many rental cars in the same place, but there is only one passenger shows up. Under this condition, only one car will be used and other cars still wait for next passenger. Therefore, we can conjecture that the electric taxi average idle time will increase.

From Figure 4.8, we know the mean value of electric taxi average idle time is not stable under Car-Sharing. We can clearly know all of the electric taxi average idle time is worse under Car-Sharing. And there is a trend in Figure 4.8. First, if the scale of electric taxi fleet increases, the electric taxi average idle time will increase. Contrary, if the scale of electric taxi fleet decreases, the electric taxi average idle time will decrease. Second, we

| Electric Taxi Number | No Car-Sharing | Car-Sharing |
|:---:|:---:|:---:|
| 5 | 0.0501 | 0.0402 |
| 6 | 0.0508 | 0.0447 |
| 7 | 0.0640 | 0.0738 |
| 8 | 0.1360 | 0.0928 |
| 9 | 0.1883 | 0.1243 |
| 10 | 0.2129 | 0.1798 |
| 11 | 0.2547 | 0.2559 |
| 12 | 0.2766 | 0.3226 |
| 13 | 0.3041 | 0.3479 |
| 14 | 0.3249 | 0.3513 |
| 15 | 0.3406 | 0.4069 |
| 16 | 0.3841 | 0.4094 |
| 17 | 0.3947 | 0.4196 |
| 18 | 0.4230 | 0.5206 |
| 19 | 0.4484 | 0.5274 |
| 20 | 0.4744 | 0.5558 |
| Mean Value | 0.2705 | 0.2921 |

**Table 4.8:** Electric taxi average idle time.

find out that if the scale of electric taxi fleet is equal to or less than 11, the electric taxi average idle time becomes lower than mean value. From Table 4.9 and Figure 4.8, we can make a brief summary: only number 11, the passenger average waiting time and electric taxi average idle time are lower than mean value. When the electric taxi number is from 5 to 10, the passenger demands is still much more than electric taxi fleet scale and rental cars. Plus rental cars are divided from the original electric taxi fleet that causes reduction of the electric taxi fleet scale. Even the electric taxi average idle time is still increasing under car-sharing; it is smaller than the value of No Car-Sharing.

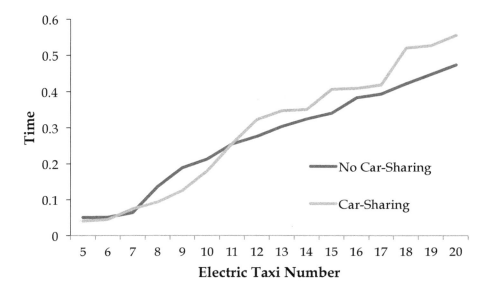

**Figure 4.8:** Electric taxi average idle time line chart.

Finally, we make a summary. Because the original electric taxi fleet is divided into two types that cause the scale of the electric taxi fleet becomes smaller than before. Even the rental car is more convenient and faster for specific passenger type, for the electric company, they will not have enough electric taxi number to satisfy other numerous passengers. Consequently, the performance measure won't correspond with our standard or mission. Obviously, introducing car-sharing management policy will negatively affect the electric taxi operation and performance. After data analysis, the electric company will stop introduce car-sharing management policy temporarily and do the further assessment.

| Electric Taxi Number | Passenger Waiting Time | Electric Taxi Average Idle Time |
|---|---|---|
| 5 | 0.1555 | 0.0402 |
| 6 | 0.1314 | 0.0447 |
| 7 | 0.1286 | 0.0738 |
| 8 | 0.1202 | 0.0928 |
| 9 | 0.1169 | 0.1243 |
| 10 | 0.1148 | 0.1798 |
| 11 | 0.1002 | 0.2559 |
| 12 | 0.0991 | 0.3226 |
| 13 | 0.0971 | 0.3479 |
| 14 | 0.0945 | 0.3513 |
| 15 | 0.0942 | 0.4069 |
| 16 | 0.0898 | 0.4094 |
| 17 | 0.0891 | 0.4196 |
| 18 | 0.0779 | 0.5206 |
| 19 | 0.0546 | 0.5274 |
| 20 | 0.0411 | 0.5558 |
| Mean Value | 0.1003 | 0.2921 |

**Table 4.9:** Passenger average waiting time and Electric taxi average idle time.

# 5

# Conclusions and Future Works

## 5.1 Conclusions

In our research, we not only construct a multi-agent simulation model. In order to approach reality, we consider the change of electric taxi speed, electric taxi power, traffic jam simulation management and so on to make our multi-agent simulation model be more credible and reliable. In addition, we provide three kinds of management policies (paths planning, car-pool and car-sharing) to observe the feasibility and efficiency to provide supervisor of taxi company as their decision-making suggestions. Following, we list the contribution that we has achieved:

First, we apply three management policies (paths planning, car-pool and car-sharing) into the electric taxi DAR operation system to observe the phenomenon and effects. We find out that apply least time as our path planning and car-pool to manage the electric taxi DAR operation system, the performance of electric taxi fleet (passenger average waiting time and electric taxi idle time) can achieve our standard. But add car-sharing into the electric taxi DAR operation system will cause the reduction of electric taxi fleet performance. So car-sharing management policy affects, even reduce the efficiency and utility of car-pool, if they are implemented in the electric taxi DAR operation system simultaneously.

Second, we have constructed a graphic user interface (GUI) for user. User can control the passenger generation rate, electric taxi fleet scale and electric station number to fit into the operation of real taxi company via our GUI. User also can make up any combination of management policies (Paths Planning, Car-Pool and Car-Sharing) to observe the result of simulation. According to the simulation result, the taxi company can modify their management policy to be more competitive and quicker response with the real condition. Our GUI also can display the electric taxi idle and passenger waiting message to let taxi company supervisor control the condition real time. We also offer a communication window between agents and user, to support the user intervene the simulation and force the agents need to interact with user to negotiate with passenger.

## 5.2    Future Works.

First, in our research and research, we consider three important performance measures: passenger average waiting time, electric taxi average idle time and electric taxi average waiting time in queue. But electric taxi company operation cost, revenue and passenger expenditure are still important performance measures. If we include these performance measures into our electric taxi DAR operation system, our simulation and data analysis will be more complete.

Second, for our GUI, we need an interaction mechanism to directly control or command electric taxis to deal with any kinds of condition in real time. In the future, we also need to construct a simulation mechanism that user is able to add or eliminate an electric taxi or passenger in the map during the simulation period. These future works can make our simulation become more flexible and valuable for simulating their condition and providing recommendation of real taxi company.

# References

1. Ali, W. (2006). *Developping 2D and 3D multi-agent geosimulation, a method and and its' application: the case of shopping behavior geosimulation in square one mall (TORONTO).* From: www.theses.ulaval.ca/2006/23343 accessed 2014.

2. Borshchev, A. and Filippov, A. (2004). From System Dynamics and Discrete Event to Practical Agent Based Modeling: Reasons, Techniques, Tools. The 22nd International Conference of the System Dynamics Society, July 25-29, 2004, Oxford, England.

3. Cordeau, J.F. and Gilbert, L.G. (2007). The dial-a-ride problem: models and algorithms. Ann Oper Res 153: pp 29–46.

4. Coslovich, L., Pesenti, R. and Ukovich, W. (2006). A two-phase insertion technique of unexpected customers for a dynamic dial-a-ride problem. European Journal of Operational Research 175: pp 1605–1615.

5. Cubillos, C., Crawford, B. and Rodríguez, N. (2007). Distributed Planning for the On-Line Dial-a-Ride Problem. Lecture Notes in Computer Science (including subseries Lecture Notes in Artificial Intelligence and Lecture Notes in Bioinformatics) 4742 LNCS:pp 160-169.

6. Cubillos, C., Polanco, F.G. and Demartini, C. (2005). Passengers Trips Planning using Contract-Net with Filters. Proceedings of the 8th International IEEE Conference on Intelligent Transportation Systems Vienna, Austria, September: pp 13-16.

7. Cubillos, C., Polanco, F.G. and Demartini, C. (2008). MADARP: A Flexible Agent Architecture for Passenger Transportation. From: http://ki.informatik. uni-wuerzburg.de/~kluegl/att2008/pdf/ accessed 2015.

8. Dubiel, B. and Tsimhoni, O. (2005). Integrating agent based modeling into a discrete event simulation. Proceedings-Winter Simulation Conference 2005, art. no. 1574355, pp:1029-1037.

9. Environment protection department, From: http://www.epd.gov. hk/epd/partner ship/chi/ tran.htm, accessed 2015.

10. Ezzedine, H., Bonte, T., Kolski, C. and Tahon, C. (2008). Integration of traffic management and traveller information systems: basic principles and case study in intermodal transport system management. International Journal of Computers, Communications & Control (IJCCC), ISSN 1841-9836, E-ISSN 1841-9844 Vol. III, No. 3:pp 281–294.

11. Ezzedine, H. and Kolski, C.(2008). Use of Petri Nets for Modeling an Agent-Based Interactive System: Basic Principles and Case Study. From: http://intechweb.org/ accessed 2015.

12. Ezzedine, H., Kolski, C. and Pe'ninou, A. (2005). Agent-oriented design of human-computer interface:application to supervision of an urban transport network. Engineering Applications of Artificial Intelligence 18: pp 255–270.

13. Ezzedine, H., Trabelsi, A. and Kolski, C. (2006). Modeling of an interactive system with an agent-based architecture using Petri nets, application of the method to the supervision of a transport system. Mathematics and Computers in Simulation 70:pp 358–376.

14. Taxicab, From: http://en.wikipedia.org/wiki/Taxicab, accessed 12 March 2015.

15. http://tw.knowledge.yahoo.com/question/question?qid=140512241 2364, accessed 2014.

16. Hunsaker, B. and Savelsbergh, M. (2002). Efficient feasibility testing for dial-a-ride problems. Operations Research Letters 30:pp169–173.

17. Ishida, T. (2002). Digital city Kyoto. Communications of the ACM 45

(7): pp 76-81.

18.    Jain, S. and McLean, C.R. (2006). A Concept Prototype for integrated gaming and simulation for incident management. Proceedings of the 2006 Winter Simulation Conference:pp 493-500.

19.    Jiang, B. (2000). Agent-based approach to modeling environment and urban systems within GIS. From: http://www.hig.se/~bjg/ accessed 2015

20.    Kok, I.d. and Lucassen, T. (2007). Using Sectors in a Multi Agent Approach to a Taxi Planning Problem. From: http://www. teunlucassen.nl/index.php accessed 2014.

21.    Lu, Q. and Dessouky, M.M. (2006). A new insertion-based construction heuristic for solving the pickup and delivery problem with time windows. European Journal of Operational Research 175:pp 672–687.

22.    Liu, Z.T., Ishida., T. and Sheng, H. (2005)Multi-agent-Based Demand Bus Simulation for Shanghai. Lecture Notes in Computer Science (including subseries Lecture Notes in Artificial Intelligence and Lecture Notes in Bioinformatics) 3446 LNAI:pp 309-322.

23.    Majid, M., Abdul, Aickelin, U. and Siebers, P. O. (2007). Human behavior modeling for discrete event and agent based simulation: A Case Study. Annual Operational Research Conference 49 (OR 49), Edinburgh, UK, pp:11-21.

24.    Martinez Moyano I J, Sallach, D., L, Bragen, M.J. and Thimmapuram, P. R. (2007). Design for a Multilayer Model of Financial Stability: Exploring the Integration of System Dynamics and Agent-based Models. From: http://www.systemdynamics.org/conferences/2007/proceed/papers/MARTI534.pdf accessed 2015.

25.    Scholl H.J. (2001). Agent-based and System Dynamics Modeling: A Call for Cross Study and Joint Research. Proceedings of the Hawaii International Conference on System Sciences, pp:62-69

26.    Seow, K.T., Dang, N.H. and Lee, D.H. (2008). Using Intelligent Collaborative Agents for Automating Distributed Taxi Dispatch. From: http://cts.cs.uic.edu/ accessed 2014.

27.    Siebers, P.O., Aickelin, U., Celia, H. and Clegg, C. (2008). Using Mul-

ti-Agent Simulation to Understand the Impact of Management Practices on Retail Performance. From: http://www.nottingham.ac.uk/cs/ accessed 2013.

28.   Taiwan Area National Freeway bureau, From: http://www.freeway.gov.tw/Defaul t.aspx, accessed 19 June 2009

29.   Taiwan environmental information, From: http://e-info.org.tw/taxonomy/term/ 17123, accessed 2014.

30.   Tsai, W.T., Fan, C., Cao, Z and Xiao, B. *et al.* (2005). A Scenario-Based Service-Oriented Rapid Multi-Agent Distributed Modeling and Simulation Framework for SoS/SOA and Its Applications. From: http://whitepapers.zdnet.co.uk/0,1000000651,260276724p,00.htm accessed 2015.

31.   Wu, C.C. (2006). Matching Models and Solution Algorithms for Urban Taxipool. From: http://etds.ncl.edu.tw/theabs/service/student_query_act.jsp accessed 2014.

32.   Zhao, J. and Dessouky, M. (2008). Service capacity design problems for mobility allowance shuttle transit systems. Transportation Research Part B 42:pp 135–146. January 2005.

33.   Wikipedia. From: http://zh.wikipedia.org/w/index.php?title=%E5%85%A8%E7%90%83%E6%9A%96%E5%8C%96&variant=zh-tw, accessed 16 May 2015.

34.   Antle, J., Apps, M., Beamish, R., Chapin, T. *et al.* (2001). Ecosystems and Their Goods and Services. From: http://www.grida.no/publications/other/ipcc_tar/?src=/climate/ipcc_tar/wg2/197.htm accessed 2015.

35.   Chao, C.C. (2009). http://www.delta-foundation.org.tw/editor/editor_detail.asp? fid=1&tpid=554. From: accessed 8 May 2015.